THE GREAT GENERALS SERIES

This distinguished series features the lives of eminent military leaders who changed history in the United States and abroad. Top military historians write concise but comprehensive biographies including the personal lives, battles, strategies, and legacies of these great generals, with the aim to provide background and insight into today's armies and wars. These books are of interest to the military history buff, and, thanks to fast-paced narratives and references to current affairs, they are also accessible to the general reader.

Patton by Alan Axelrod

Grant by John Mosier

Eisenhower by John Wukovits

LeMay by Barrett Tillman

MacArthur by Richard B. Frank

Stonewall Jackson by Donald A. Davis

Bradley by Alan Axelrod

Pershing by Jim Lacey

Andrew Jackson by Robert V. Remini

Sherman by Steven E. Woodworth

Robert E. Lee by Noah Andre Trudeau

Washington by Gerald M. Carbone

Custer by Duane Schultz

Marshall

Lessons in Leadership

H. Paul Jeffers

with

Alan Axelrod

palgrave
macmillan

MARSHALL
Copyright © H. Paul Jeffers, Alan Axelrod 2010.
All rights reserved.

First published in 2010 by PALGRAVE MACMILLAN® in the US–a
division of St. Martin's Press LLC, 175 Fifth Avenue, New York, NY
10010.

Palgrave® and Macmillan® are registered trademarks in the United
States, the United Kingdom, Europe and other countries.

ISBN-13: 978-0-230-61416-1

Design by Letra Libre

Printed in the United States of America.

Contents

Foreword

GEORGE C. MARSHALL'S WAS THE VISION, THE SKILL, AND THE FORCE behind the American victory in World War II. His legacy has powerfully driven the Army for the sixty-five years since. George Catlett Marshall, who never led troops in battle, became the most powerful U.S. military officer of the twentieth century.

This excellent biography by H. Paul Jeffers—written during the months before his death in December 2009 with contributions by Alan Axelrod—is laid out as clearly and directly as it can be. A young man from a solid family, George Marshall decided he wanted to go to the Virginia Military Institute, fell in love with the U.S. Army, and stuck with it through hardship and challenge for the next forty-six years of his life. His extraordinary mental acuity, thoughtful personality, and inner resolution took him to the pinnacle of armed forces leadership in the U.S. Armed Forces, and beyond. After his military career, he served as secretary of state, a position in which he conceived and drove forward the plan for post–World War II European recovery, which came to be known as the Marshall Plan. His public career culminated in his appointment as secretary of defense during the darkest days of the Korean War, when he presided over the relief for insubordination of his old comrade and rival, General of the Army Douglas MacArthur.

━━━

The outlines of that story are well known, but so remarkable that they bear retelling. Yet Jeffers and Axelrod have done more; they have taken us into the young Marshall's life for the glimpses of his personality and character which formed the basis for all he achieved. As a young man, Marshall had about him a certain temperament and judgment that won the respect of his peers at the Virginia Military Institute. He learned discipline, and hard work, and he carried within him a kind of "moral force" that moved him and everyone around him. Shortly after graduating from VMI, he personally sought appointments with the nation's leaders, including the president of the United States, to gain permission to take the examination which, if he passed, would earn him a commission in the U.S. Army. It was an indication of his forceful character that would surface again and again.

As a lieutenant commanding troops in the Philippines, he was a stickler for discipline and sound organization. He was a leader, not a politician seeking support from his troops, as others were. And he was a teacher, instructing first at VMI and later at the Army school at Fort Leavenworth. Still later, entrusted to planning major maneuvers, he proved without equal in the brilliance of his planning and organization. Although he had not seen combat, his service in the United States and in the Philippines had earned him an army-wide reputation.

It took all his politicking to gain a foothold in the American Expeditionary Force (AEF) headed to France when the United States entered World War I in 1917. Soon he was at the very center of the action as Pershing's fastest-rising officer, preparing the first American forces for combat in France. Marshall learned the battlefield, and learned that it ran much deeper and wider than where bullets flew. He also showed his character when he, as a mere major, stood up against an unjust critique by General Pershing himself. It certainly added to his reputation, giving it a mythological character almost always exclusively reserved for commanders in the thick of desperate battle. But he also displayed a temper. In time, it too would become the stuff of legend, but, for the present, his impatient grousing blew back against him and delayed his advancement.

Nevertheless, he was in France and he was the key planner on General Pershing's staff, responsible for the operations and logistics of more than 1.2 million American soldiers. Myth, legend, character, and temperament aside, Marshall proved himself a star, orchestrating the maneuvers and support of the major U.S. actions that brought the Allies victory in World War I.

Persevering through the cutbacks and humiliations of the interwar years, Marshall saw service in the United States and China, including an important leadership position in the Infantry School at Fort Benning, Georgia. And it was here that he began to compile the document on which so much World War II history would depend, his "Black Book," in which he inscribed the names of those whom he would later pick for high level command in World War II.

Eventually, in 1938, he rose to the position of deputy army chief of staff, and with World War II under way in Europe, was subsequently selected to be the chief of staff, charged with building an army and mobilizing millions of troops and forming the forces that would wage war in two global theaters. Unfortunately, Marshall's genius in this role—and genius it was—has mostly laid concealed in the maze of bureaucratic warfare that marks the Pentagon and the civil military interface in Washington. This biography hits the high points well, and relates them to the major action in the field, but the full range of Marshall's achievement bears emphasizing here. Because his work was behind battle lines, it has been largely masked from the public.

Among Marshall's most important contributions were his advocacy of the Europe-first approach in a war that, as far as the American public was concerned, had begun in the Pacific; his selection of major commanders, like Dwight Eisenhower; his advocacy of what are now known as "joint" and "combined operations," in which the Army works seamlessly with other services and allies; his steadfast focus on the cross-Channel invasion of France; and his supremely difficult decision to halt replacement flows to Europe in the midst of their tough battles in order to build up the strength to invade Japan.

The "how" of these contributions is of course critical. Marshall may have been the army chief of staff, but he was subordinate to the secretary of war and the president, enmeshed in a joint services bureaucracy, reliant on a difficult international alliance and, inevitably, part of the highly political Roosevelt administration. He had to move adroitly, gathering facts, authorizing studies, working with others. He was admired and respected by members of Congress and the administration, but was not above their authorities and judgments. And, unfortunately, much of the "how" is simply beyond the scope of this biography. From personal experience, I can tell you that staff work doesn't always make exciting reading, however challenging it is to the staff officers themselves. But it is demanding and brutalizing work—twenty-hour days, much back-and-forth, reputations made and lost, friends made, and sometimes, enemies as well. Facts count for much, but friendships and alliances can be decisive. Much happens behind the stolid walls of the Pentagon, and across the glassy waters of the Potomac whose effects surface months and years later.

Still, what does come through in this book are the most visible, immediate, and consequential results of Marshall's critical tenure, and the writers have done an admirable job of capturing the man's attributes and character as revealed in his major decisions. His deft handling of temperamental commanders like Patton and MacArthur, his interface at the political levels with Roosevelt, Secretary of War Henry Stimson and Prime Minister Winston Churchill, and above all the integrity and moral courage he demonstrated in dealings with Allied officers and the tough strategic issues of the war.

When Marshall took on his postwar responsibilities, he descended into a highly charged political environment. Sent on a mission to resolve the civil war in China between the Nationalists and the Communists, he, of course, failed. That is the inevitable outcome of inherently hopeless missions. The situation was simply irresolvable, given the circumstances, the narrow extent of Marshall's authority, and the limitations on U.S. resources available for commitment. But Marshall was the man President Truman had put out front, and Marshall absorbed much of the blame for the failure. He therefore assumed leadership of the department of state and, later, the department of defense under a cloud. And though he provided the strong leadership needed for the critical first year of the Korean War, he was also "used-up" politically in the process. It is a sad but true fact of American democracy that even great military leaders often suffer hard knocks after reverting to participation in the political process, elective or appointed.

By the standards of the military profession, Marshall ranks at the very top: a brilliant planner and organizer, a strategist, a wartime leader who guided the U.S. military to victory in its greatest war. His standards and approach pervade the Army to this day. Marshall saw it as a learning and teaching organization imbued with the highest standards of discipline and integrity. For him, the Army had to function as a team player in joint and combines operations. Looking to Marshall's example, the officer corps is ennobled by his indelible pattern of patient, humble, selfless service. The forces that fought and are fighting successfully on the ground in Korea, Vietnam, Iraq, and Afghanistan, today continue to bear and benefit from the legacy of George Catlett Marshall.

—*General Wesley K. Clark (Ret.)*

Introduction

ON NOVEMBER 14, 1938, PRESIDENT FRANKLIN D. ROOSEVELT invited Assistant Secretary of the Army Louis A. Johnson and others—including the army's chief of staff, General Malin Craig and his new deputy, George C. Marshall—to the White House. FDR wanted to discuss military appropriations, a subject very much on Marshall's mind because, in assessing the preparedness of the army in case it had to go to war, he had discovered that it was woefully unready in every aspect. While the second great war of the twentieth century would soon begin in Europe and Japan was at war with China—already, millions of men were fighting—the army of the still-neutral United States consisted of fewer than 200,000 officers and enlisted men scattered over 130 posts, camps, and stations, with an Air Corps of only sixty-two tactical squadrons. Equipment that had been marginally modern at the conclusion of the Great War in 1918 was now largely obsolescent, even obsolete. During the postwar period, relentless congressional paring of appropriations and the Great Depression had reduced the army to that of a third-rate power. Among world armies, it ranked seventeenth in strength.[1]

Marshall came to the meeting thoroughly persuaded that bolstering American readiness for war required a balanced building of both the army and the Army Air Corps. Roosevelt, however, proposed a dramatic expansion of air power by 15,000 planes, but no enlargement of the army. He turned to the new deputy chief of staff for agreement: "Don't you think so, George?"

Marshall was new in Washington, and he was clearly moving up, one step away from becoming chief of staff, the army's senior officer. Anyone else in this position would have simply agreed with the commander in chief. Instead, Marshall replied, "Mr. President, I'm sorry, I don't agree with that at all."[2]

The response was stunningly brusque, an effect that was as much a product of Marshall's distaste for anyone, even the president, addressing him informally by his first name as it was the result of profound disagreement. A startled Roosevelt looked at Marshall coolly and abruptly ended the meeting.

Leaving the White House that day, Marshall supposed that by speaking so bluntly to Roosevelt he had no future in Washington. But that was before Harry L. Hopkins, FDR's secretary of commerce and most trusted adviser, got to know him. The first time Hopkins called the War Department and asked to come over to meet with the deputy chief of staff about increasing the army's budget, Marshall insisted instead on going to Hopkins at his Commerce Department office. This gesture of courtesy began an alliance between the two men that prompted Hopkins not only to persuade Roosevelt to become more amenable to the army's needs, but to champion Marshall as General Malin Craig's successor.

Marshall was again summoned to the White House on Sunday afternoon, April 23, 1939. He was shown into the president's second-floor study, where he found Roosevelt happily seated amid stacks of stamp albums and dealers' catalogues. Two years older than Marshall, Roosevelt was a navy man at heart. In his youth, he had spent summers on yachts off the coast of Maine and in the Great War he had been assistant secretary of the navy. (During a recent discussion of the armed services' needs, Marshall pointed out the presidential bias by interrupting him with the plea, "At least, Mr. President, stop speaking of the Army as 'they' and the Navy as 'us.'"[3]) The president looked up from his stamp albums and said, "General Marshall"—he had learned to drop the familiar "George"—"I have it in mind to choose you as the next Chief of Staff of the United States Army. What do you think about that?"

Ahead of Lieutenant General George C. Marshall in seniority were twenty-one major generals and eleven brigadiers, most of whom had political connections in positions to lobby on their behalf in the War Department and at the White House. Any other officer in his position would have simply thanked his president for the unexpected honor, but Marshall replied,

"Nothing, Mr. President, except to remind you that I have the habit of saying exactly what I think. And that, as you know, can often be unpleasing. Is that all right?"

Grinning, Roosevelt replied, "Yes."

"I have to remind you again, it may be unpleasant."

Still smiling, Roosevelt said, "I know."[4]

CHAPTER 1

The Beast

THE THIRD CHILD AND SECOND SON OF GEORGE C. MARSHALL AND the former Laura Emily Bradford, George Catlett Marshall Jr. was born on December 31, 1880, in Uniontown, Pennsylvania. He grew up telling teachers that he was certifiably descended from John Marshall, the fourth chief justice of the United States. To other boys he bragged about being related to the dreaded pirate Blackbeard. How he acquired the nickname "Flicker" is unclear, but it could have evolved from a distortion of the word "Freckles." As a redhead, he had them in abundance. Young George liked licorice candy that he bought at Crane's store and enjoyed reading the adventures of Jesse James and other cowboys in dime novels, along with tales of Nick Carter, Diamond Dick, and Frank Merriwell, and the "Old Sleuth" series. In the small-town America described by Mark Twain in *The Adventures of Tom Sawyer,* George Marshall was more like Huckleberry Finn than Tom. He found school-learning hard and was deemed "slow" by many.

George never emulated Huck by floating down a river on a raft, but he did attempt to build one. His purpose was to open a shortcut to school by starting a ferry service at a penny per trip across a stream called Coal Lick Run that flowed behind the Marshalls' house. When his effort to build the raft failed, a local shopkeeper assisted his enterprise by giving him an old flat-bottomed boat. For several days, George's ferry business thrived. One day a group of girls informed him they were out of pennies for the fare. Demanding free passage, they boarded the boat. When he refused service, they started to ridicule his poor performance as a student.

"I was terribly humiliated," Marshall recalled many years later in an interview with Forrest C. Pogue, his official biographer, "and what made it worse, my chum Andy [Thompson] began laughing at me. And there I was—the girls in the flatboat all jeering at me and my engineer and boon companion laughing at me and I was stuck. Just then my eye fastened on a cork in the floor of the boat which was utilized in draining it. With the inspiration of the moment, I pulled the cork, and under the pressure of the weight of the passengers a stream of water shot up in the air. All the girls screamed, and I sank the boat in the middle of the stream."[1]

Forced to wade ashore, with dresses soaked and mud-stained, the frantic girls ran home and reported the disaster to their mothers. Irate, the women sought redress from George Sr. The result for George Jr. was punishment with a hickory switch in the cellar.

━━◈━━

Looking back on his schooldays, George evoked a painful time when he felt ashamed to admit his ignorance, particularly in arithmetical problems. "If it was history, I was all right; I could star in history," he recalled. "But the other things I was very, very poor in. Grammar I knew nothing about."[2]

Unlike his older brother Stuart and his sister Marie, George was seen by their father as a disappointment. Six years older, Stuart Bradford Marshall possessed all the admirable traits of diligent application and ambition that their father had exhibited to succeed in business and that seemed to be missing in George Junior. Poor marks for schoolwork or a report of classroom misdemeanors meant a display of parental dismay in the form of the dreaded hickory.

Part owner of a coal company with 150 coke ovens and coal fields, George C. Marshall Sr. was a man of his times. A respected businessman and a vestryman of St. Peter's Episcopal Church, he was a Freemason and Knight Templar as well as a proud Democrat who heartily backed Grover Cleveland for president in the year George Jr. was born, and again in 1888. He was for William Jennings Bryan in 1896 and took George Jr. to march in a pro-Bryan parade. Wearing a gray paper hat and carrying a cane, George Sr. approved of the way the Republican President William McKinley's choice to be assistant secretary of the navy, Theodore Roosevelt, spoke out about driving the Spanish out of Cuba, even if it took the navy and army to do it.

Originally from Kentucky, George C. Marshall, Sr. had seen some action in the Civil War as a rifleman in a brisk skirmish in the town of Augusta, Kentucky, on the Ohio River opposite (and east of) Cincinnati, Ohio. Because its residents were almost equally divided in their allegiance between North and South, the city council raised a militia early in the war to protect the community from whatever side might threaten its peace and security. Eager to help, and hoping to impress Laura Bradford, the pretty, fifteen-year-old daughter of a locally prominent landowner, sixteen-year-old George volunteered. When a detachment of Confederate cavalry led by Colonel Basil Duke, George's cousin, arrived on September 27, 1862, to occupy the town, a battle ensued. When it ended, the Confederates had suffered twenty-one killed and eighteen wounded and the town's militia, seven dead and fifteen wounded. To ensure no further trouble, Duke ordered immediately after the battle one hundred militiamen be held as hostages, including George Marshall. When he was released a few weeks later, he found Laura Bradford more impressed with his heroics than were her parents.

Because the Marshalls had little standing in Augusta, the prominent Bradfords discouraged Laura from seriously considering George as a suitor. They managed to stall Laura and George's marriage for a decade, but, finally, in 1873, the couple married and left Kentucky for the coal- and steel-making region of western Pennsylvania. Here they settled in Uniontown, where George Marshall soon prospered. Their first child lived only six months. The next, a son, Stuart, became the father's favorite. He was followed by a daughter, Marie, and then George Jr., who became the mother's favorite. The future general remembered his wife as very quiet, but with a great deal of strength of character and a keen sense of humor.

Recalling a mother who was always forgiving, Marshall told biographer Forrest Pogue, "Sometimes she may have been worried; sometimes she may have been ashamed; sometimes she may have been shocked; but she heard what the matter was, what the affair was, and whenever there was humor in it, it amused her very much."[3]

George Jr. could never remember exactly when he started thinking about a military career. He might have overheard his mother say something about the virtues of soldiering to his father after a conversation with a distant relative, Colonel Charles Marshall of Baltimore, who had been at Robert E. Lee's side in the Civil War. Shortly thereafter the decision was announced by Mr. Marshall that eldest son Stuart was to enter the Virginia Military Institute (VMI). Part of the impetus for this choice, instead of West Point, lay in an abrupt downturn in the family's finances because of a failed investment. Although the United States Military Academy was tuition-free, George Sr. was a prominent Democrat, and appointments to West Point were made by congressmen or senators, all of whom in the Pennsylvania delegation at that time happened to be Republicans. Although Stuart performed well in the military classes at VMI, his real interests lay in science. Rather than following graduation in 1894 with an application for a commission in the U.S. Army, he joined a local ironworks as a chemist.

Seeing Stuart in a cadet's uniform and hearing him talk about his VMI experiences may have influenced George's decision to enroll at the Institute, but his decision actually to pursue a military career seems to have resulted from his seeing the triumphal return to Uniontown of Company C of the Tenth Pennsylvania Infantry from the Philippines in 1899. Marshall was impressed by the parade and celebration, a grand American small-town demonstration of pride in Uniontown's young men and of wholesome enthusiasm over their achievements.

Painfully remembering his second son's struggles in public schools, George Sr. nurtured grave reservations about George Jr.'s ability to succeed in the military. His doubts were exacerbated by Stuart's objections. Having done very well at VMI, he stated that he was fearful his brother would do poorly and disgrace the family name. The expression of concern was directed not to George Sr. but to Mrs. Marshall because she would be paying the costs of George's tuition ($365) and uniforms ($70) out of the proceeds of sales of real estate properties in Augusta and Uniontown. Overhearing Stuart's harsh words, General Marshall later said, made more of an impression on him than all his instructors, parental pressures, or any other factor. He decided right then and there that, in the slang of the period, he was going to "wipe" Stuart's face by excelling as a cadet at VMI.

Venturing away from home for the first time, sixteen-year-old George C. Marshall Jr. arrived in the village of Lexington, Virginia, on September 11, 1897, and climbed a steep hill to stand at the edge of the broad parade ground on which Stonewall Jackson had drilled cadets when he was an instructor at VMI in the 1850s. Stuart said that the spirit of the Confederate hero was so great throughout the institute that an eerie light was seen at times in his old classroom. Far more stern and foreboding to Marshall was the figure of the present superintendent, General Scott Shipp.

Six feet tall, lean, shy, and getting over a bout of typhoid fever, George Marshall was assigned to barracks room 88. As he walked down a long avenue toward the building, he heard a bugle sound assembly for dress parade. Watching the adjutant and sergeant strutting out to form the line on which the battalion would fall in, he thought they were wonderful-looking figures.

Although Superintendent Shipp had banned the hazing of freshmen, called "rats," George and other first-year students were subjected to a ritual that required them to bare their buttocks and squat for ten minutes over a bayonet, the handle of which had been jammed into the floor. Some witnesses averred that he did so for twenty minutes, but because he was still weak and recuperating from typhoid this seems doubtful. When his strength at last gave out, he rose shakily. Brushing against the bayonet, he was cut and bled profusely, but because all who had participated in the hazing could have been expelled for violating Shipp's ban, he did not report the incident.

At the end of the year, his academic standing proved that he was not as "slow" as his brother had feared. Of eighty-two men in his class, Marshall ranked eighteenth, with his strongest showing in the military classes. As a reward, he was named first corporal for the following term.

After a summer at home, Marshall in his second year again fared best in military subjects and finished the year ranked twenty-fifth academically in a class of sixty-nine. A civil engineering major, he completed the third year ranked nineteenth among forty-seven and was unanimously elected "first captain," making him the highest-ranking cadet officer.

"What I learned most at VMI," Marshall recalled, "was self-control, discipline, and the problem of managing men which fell to the cadet noncommissioned officer and cadet officer. He was very severely judged by his classmates if he was slack."[4]

In his senior year, George C. Marshall Jr. could have been the model for the can-do heroes of books by Horatio Alger and articles in *Boys' Life, The Saturday Evening Post,* and other magazines that celebrated the all-American-boy with the "bully" attitude and spirit extolled by Vice President Theodore "Teddy" Roosevelt, who felt that (as he wrote in his 1900 essay "Character and Success") "in the great battle of life, no brilliancy of intellect, no perfection of bodily development, would count when weighed in the balance" against the combination of moral qualities that create character.

At twenty years old, Marshall was tall, handsome, a tackle on the VMI football team, drill field leader, and sufficiently well respected to have been chosen to lead the Ring Dance at the Ring Figure Ball. He was also head over heels in love. The object of his affections was the beautiful, auburn-haired belle of Lexington whose only flaw was a heart condition that limited her physical activities to countryside outings and drives around the road that bounded the drill field. A doctor's daughter, she resided in a wooden Gothic-style cottage with her widowed mother at 319 Letcher Avenue at the Limit Gate of the campus.

Passing by on a spring day with a friend, Marshall heard one of his mother's favorite tunes playing on a piano. Looking for the source of the music, he peered through an open window and found Elizabeth Carter Coles at the keyboard. Inquiring from the friend and other cadets, he learned she was called Lily. Delighting in flirting with VMI men, she had already disappointed several who asked to marry her. One of them, Marshall learned, was his brother.

When Stuart made unkind, unfair remarks about her, perhaps because she had rejected him, Marshall was reported to have told his goddaughter, Rose Page Wilson, years later, "I cut him off my list."[5] He remained estranged from Stuart for the rest of his life.

Noting that Lily's family ancestry included a governor of Virginia and a member of the Continental Congress at the time of the Declaration of Independence, and that other relatives were among the finest names in the landed gentry of Virginia, Marshall recalled that Lily's family looked down on him because the name of his hometown sounded as if it had been founded during or after the Civil War. They were shocked when they discovered that Uniontown, Pennsylvania—founded on July 4, 1776—was actually a year older than Lexington, Virginia.

As graduation approached, Marshall found that the odds favoring a VMI graduate's obtaining a commission to make him the equal of a new graduate of West Point had improved greatly with an authorization by Congress to the army to expand army strength by 100,000 enlisted men and 1,200 officers to put down an insurrection in the Philippines related to the Spanish-American War. Of these new officers, one-fifth were to be selected by means of a written examination. Although Marshall's parents were against his choice of an army career, George Sr. recognized that his second son's whole heart was in it and wrote to Superintendent Shipp to ask if George had the qualifications essential to the making of an officer. Shipp said he had complete confidence that if commissioned in the army, Marshall, would measure above the average West Pointer.

Given this assurance, Mr. Marshall wrote to a VMI graduate, John S. Wise, who was close to President McKinley, to appeal to the president in support of George's application for permission to take the qualifying examination. Noting that George was related to Chief Justice John Marshall and that George bore the name most worthily, Wise heartily recommended him.

To increase the likelihood of being granted permission to take the test, Marshall traveled to the nation's capital carrying letters of recommendation from John Wise and Superintendent Shipp. Demonstrating the pluck that Teddy Roosevelt so admired in American youths, Marshall sought and obtained required endorsements by showing up unexpectedly at the office of Attorney General Philander Knox, who was a friend of George Sr., and at the home of the chairman of the House Military Affairs Committee, John A. Hull. Both were polite but promised nothing. Marshall rounded out his Washington odyssey by seeking out the commander in chief himself. Arriving at the White House, he was informed by the butler that without an appointment he would never meet with the president. Undaunted, he waited in the foyer and watched people who had appointments go into the presidential office. When a man and his daughter were escorted in by the butler, Marshall attached himself to the procession and entered the president's office. After the pair had met with the chief executive, Marshall found himself alone with

McKinley. The president asked him what he wanted, and Marshall calmly stated his case.

"I don't recall what he [President McKinley] said," Marshall noted in an interview more than half a century later, "but from that [meeting] I think flowed my appointment or rather my authority to appear for examination."[6]

On September 6, 1901, as McKinley was shaking hands in a reception line in the Temple of Music at the Pan-American Exposition in Buffalo, New York, an anarchist, Leon Czolgosz, shot him at point-blank range. Eight days later, the president died, and Vice President Theodore Roosevelt succeeded to office. On that very day, Marshall reported to Governors Island in New York Harbor to begin the three-day examination. He found it surprisingly easy, scoring an average of 84.8, but did concede to Shipp that he had difficulty with the geography questions.

Guarding against the possibility of failing to obtain a commission, Marshall had accepted appointment as commandant and instructor at the Danville Military Institute in Virginia. Taking up his post at the military elementary and prep school, he taught arithmetic, algebra, history, English, and drill regulations and discipline while waiting to hear if he would become, as Wise jokingly wrote to a member of the examining board, one of the fittest pieces of food for gunpowder turned out by VMI for many years. Informed that he would receive his army commission as second lieutenant on December 31, his twenty-first birthday, Marshall called the news a very acceptable Christmas present, resigned from his teaching position, and decided to propose to Lily.

Confirmed as a second lieutenant on January 13, 1902, George Catlett Marshall Jr. received orders to report to the newly organized Thirtieth Infantry Regiment at Fort Myer, Virginia, on February 13. He was sworn in by a notary public on February 3. Eight days later, he and Lily were married in an evening ceremony in the parlor of the Coles cottage in the presence of his parents, his sister Marie, brother Stuart (despite their estrangement), best friend Andy Thompson (from the flatboat days), Lily's mother and brother, various Coles relatives, and friends. The bride and groom left Lexington in the morning by train for Washington. Rather than requiring him to report to the regiment that day, a sympathetic officer told him that he was being granted a five-day leave for a honeymoon. Staying at the New Willard Hotel on Pennsylvania Avenue, Second Lieutenant and Mrs. Marshall made a handsome couple, but the bliss he expected was tempered by disappointment when his beautiful new bride said that because of her delicate heart condition she could never risk bearing children. On February 8, Marshall kissed Lily good-bye at Union Station. As a train took her back to Lexington, he reported to Fort Myer and remained five days, followed by a three-week stay at Fort Slocum, New York. Sent with seven other officers on a troop train to San Francisco, he was quartered at the Presidio. On April 12 he boarded the army transport *Kilpatrick* bound for the Philippines.

By the time the ship arrived in the great cluster of large and small islands that the United States had officially wrested from Spain, the fight to suppress an insurrection by natives—the mission from which Company C of the Tenth Pennsylvania Infantry had in 1899 returned to a stirring salute from the people of Uniontown—was largely over. An army of 70,000 men under General Arthur MacArthur had been reduced to 42,000 under a civilian government in Manila headed by Governor William Howard Taft. Rebel holdouts on the large island of Luzon, primarily in the Batangas area, had been defeated by troops under Brigadier General Benjamin Franklin Bell only a few weeks before Marshall sailed from San Francisco. Assigned to Company G of the Thirtieth Infantry, the newlywed lieutenant arrived at the village of Calapan on the island of Mindoro. Having grown up in the temperate climate and rolling countryside of western Pennsylvania and come of age on VMI's manicured drill field atop a Lexington hill, Marshall suddenly had to deal with stifling heat in a village hacked out of fetid jungle and infested not only with insects and snakes, but guerrilla fighters. Called *insurrectos,* they made no distinction between shooting a Spaniard and shooting an American. Neither had Uniontown or Lexington ever been ravaged by a cholera epidemic. Visiting a camp for isolating the stricken, Marshall found the soldiers peacefully eating their suppers on coffins.

In manning a ferry on Coal Lick Run he never had a problem like the one that confronted him at a stream while leading a seven-man patrol on a small island where a band of *insurrectos* had been reported. The trouble began when they encountered natives trying to save the life of a pony that had been attacked by a crocodile. "They were just sewing him up without any regard to the pony's feelings," he recalled, "and that horrified the men."

With Marshall leading, the soldiers waded single-file into the narrow stream.

"They were behind me," Marshall related, "and they were holding their rifles up and their ammunition belts up to keep them clear from the water. When we got about two-thirds of the way across, there was a splash up above us and one fellow yelled, 'Crocodile.' In about a second they all plunged ahead. They ran over me. I was ground right down to the bottom. Their feet went up my back and over me and up the other side. I finally came to the surface pretty well done up."

Faced with a situation unanticipated by VMI lectures and officers' guidebooks, he climbed a steep bank where his seven dripping, panicked men were standing and looking very guilty and very uncertain of themselves. Standing in front of them, wet and covered with mud, he realized that he had not only to reinstate military order, but to restore their soldierly bearing and self-esteem. He called them to attention, commanded "Right shoulder arms," and marched them back into the water. When they reached the opposite bank, he ordered them to return across the stream. After he inspected them and their rifles, they were indeed soldierly as they resumed their excursion into the mountains in search of the elusive *insurrectos*.

Reflecting on the incident sixty years later, and noting that neither he nor any of the men ever referred to it again, he said, "I thought afterwards that I had done what I think was just about the right thing. It wasn't a time for cussing around."[7]

Straight from civilian life, having only VMI classes and textbooks as guides, he found himself marking his twenty-second birthday as virtually the governor of the southern end of Mindoro Island in an army that consisted of hurriedly made officers, enlisted ranks of all sorts and conditions, and a seemingly endless number of forms to file that left him an expert on the handling of papers. These factors made service in the Philippines quite trying, he noted later, but they were also developing elements of personal character instilled in boyhood and at VMI, laying the foundation for a career in the military, and teaching him that an army's success rests on the work of its staff officers.

He also came to understand the plight of the enlisted man. One day while working in a torrential rain, a tall, lanky soldier from the mountains of Kentucky paused in the middle of a shoveling job, looked up at a supervising sergeant, and grumbled, "I didn't see nothing like this in that damned recruiting circular."

"Keep your mouth shut and shovel," barked the sergeant. "That's your job."

Marshall recalled, "That gave me a lasting impression of the Regular Army, what discipline meant, what dependability meant in times of difficulty."

A captain who observed Marshall in the Philippines and would serve under him in World War II as a general found the youthful Marshall just about the most self-contained lieutenant he ever met in the U.S. Army. Walter Kreuger found that Marshall had a sagacity and thoughtfulness beyond his years.

After witnessing American soldiers burn down a cathedral containing a religious library in reprisal for guerrilla attacks, he opined that the men should be court-martialed. Turning to an astonished Kreuger, he explained, "There is a beast in every fighting man which begins tugging at its chains, and a good officer must learn how to keep the beast under control, both in his men and himself."[8]

Near the end of October 1903, Marshall's service with the Thirtieth Infantry ended with the arrival of elements of the Seventh Infantry and orders to board the U.S. Army transport USS *Sherman* for passage home. Marshall's personal orders said his next post was Fort Reno in the Oklahoma Territory. Arriving on Christmas Day, he began what he would later regard as his formal military education.

CHAPTER 2

Junior Officer

AFTER EIGHTEEN MONTHS OF CONTENDING WITH RAIN, MUD, AND threats from *insurrectos* in the Philippine jungles, in late 1903 Second Lieutenant George C. Marshall suddenly found himself in an army that had no enemy. He had come from soldiering in the field to a spit and polish army of garrison routines at Fort Reno in the Oklahoma Territory. A relic of westward expansion, the former post was named by the Civil War general and Indian fighter Philip Henry Sheridan in honor of a friend and wartime comrade, Major General Jesse L. Reno, killed at the Civil War battle of South Mountain (Maryland) in 1862. Composed of sixteen square miles of Oklahoma Territory along the Canadian River, Fort Reno had been chosen as a cavalry post for the purpose of quelling Cheyenne and Arapaho uprisings, but by November 1903 that danger had long since ended, leaving Marshall and the rest of the Fort Reno garrison to face the tedium and harsh climate of the southern plains. In some ways, these were enemy enough. Certainly they prevented Lily Coles Marshall, with her delicate health, from joining her husband, who settled into austere bachelors' quarters.

Although his wife was not at his side, she and her widowed mother, living together back in Lexington, were financially dependent upon him. In addition to looking after their needs, Marshall (as an officer and a gentleman) also had to pay for his own uniforms, saber, revolver, field glasses, bedding, mess kit, and civilian clothes—all on a monthly salary of $116.67. As he recalled for his official biographer, "I had to keep track down to the last dime."[1]

Three months after arriving at Fort Reno, Marshall was appointed the post ordnance officer, and in June he took on the additional duty of engineer officer. He also enrolled in a fort school set up as part of Secretary of War Elihu Root's program to improve the quality of the officer corps. Marshall passed examinations in military topography, field engineering, security and information (later known as battlefield intelligence), "Troops in Campaign," and international law. Although the idea of educating officers while they served was progressive, the courses themselves were founded on outdated doctrines and tactics of the Civil War and Spanish-American War, in which the infantry was coordinated with cavalry, as represented by a class in "Horses, Saddles and Bridles."

+>——+—<+

In June 1905, after a year and a half of garrison duty at Fort Reno, Marshall found himself on a list of ten officers from the Oklahoma Territory temporarily assigned to Fort Clark, Texas (about a hundred miles west of San Antonio), to assist in the mapping of 2,000 square miles in the southwestern part of the state. His area was to be just west of Del Rio, a two-day march from Fort Clark. Although he thought it all too typical of the army to send an infantryman to the headquarters of the First Cavalry, the assignment resulted in his first encounter with the man who thirty-four years later would recommend him to be his successor as army chief of staff.

Not that the first meeting with Malin Craig, in 1905, was in any way auspicious. Marshall would later call the mapping assignment the hardest service he'd ever had in the army. When Captain Craig met him, he concluded from Marshall's ragged appearance that he couldn't possibly be an officer, and instead addressed Marshall's sergeant. The fact is that Marshall had just been through a lot. He had set out from Fort Clark across an arid tract with two riding horses, a wagon, a four-line mule team, and a surveying team of two soldiers and a civilian, all bound for the town of Langtry. Originally built as a camp by Southern Pacific track layers, the rough-and-ready town was named for a railway executive, George Langtry, and more than locally famous as the home of Judge Roy Bean, the self-proclaimed "Law West of the Pecos," who died in 1903. Marshall's team had to work in heat that reached 130 degrees, with Marshall walking the railroad track and measuring distance by counting rail sections. It was both tedious and strenuous, but the modern military ran on railroads, and a precise survey was necessary to efficient logistics, tactics, and strategy. But then the food started running low, and for a long while only bacon and canned beans were left to eat. Marshall suffered from heartburn so painful he could barely drink without gasping. The surveying party moved ten or fifteen miles a day for fifty miles, at one point enduring an eighteen-hour stretch with no water.

When Marshall and his men reached Langtry at the end of July, they found a month's pay awaiting them. After his sergeant announced to the men of the town that all the women in the local bordello were being commandeered by the army, Marshall had to act quickly and diplomatically to avert a riot by persuading both the sergeant and the outraged male population of Langtry to accept a sharing arrangement.

After taking on supplies and other refreshment at Langtry, the mapping detail headed north and eastward to Fort Clark, arriving at the end of August. Marshall had lost nearly thirty pounds, was sunburned, and sported a shredded Panama hat that had been chewed by a mule. This was the condition he was in when he first met Captain Malin Craig. Craig was thus unimpressed by the cover, but once he learned more about the book, he changed his mind. Marshall's superiors declared his map the best they had received and the only complete one of seven drawn by ten teams. As a reward, Marshall was granted four months' leave.[2]

His Uniontown homecoming was bittersweet. The house he had grown up in had been torn down to make room for a movie theater, and his parents had moved to a new eleven-story building with offices and apartments called the "Skyscraper." As he walked the streets of a town grown unfamiliar, he happened upon Trip, a friend's pet terrier who had been one of Marshall's own closest companions in youth. The dog didn't recognize him. Marshall left Uniontown for Estmont in Albemarle County, Virginia, where Lily had been summering with relatives, and, despite her fragile health, she decided to accompany her husband back to Fort Reno—along with her mother.

⊨══╡

Back in Oklahoma after his four-months' leave, in the spring of 1906 Marshall learned that he was the only Fort Reno officer who had expressed an interest in attending the Infantry and Cavalry School at Fort Leavenworth. Established by order of General William T. Sherman in 1881 and reorganized several times, the school had been suspended for four years after the Spanish-American War because of the heavy demands created by the army's occupation of the Philippines. In his 1901 report, Secretary of War Elihu Root noted that more than one-third of all the officers in the army had been without any opportunity for systematic study of the science of war and therefore recommended reestablishing the school. The War Department directed that the infantry and cavalry school at Fort Leavenworth should be enlarged and developed into a general service and staff college for all arms of the service. When the reorganized school opened on September 1, 1902, with General J. Franklin Bell as commandant, three separate schools had been established, including the infantry and cavalry school. The method of selecting the student officers was changed so that none could be admitted with a rank lower than captain. Although Marshall had twice scored highest in annual competitions to qualify for what he called the Leavenworth detail, he found that the assignment always went to a higher-ranking officer, none of whom did well at all, and all of whom came back disgruntled and critical of the Leavenworth system. In 1906, Marshall was the only one who wanted to go and was therefore admitted by default.

Marshall moved to Kansas alone, but as soon as married officers' quarters became available, Lily and her mother joined him at Fort Leavenworth. He found himself the youngest of fifty-four students, all of whom were higher in rank and had many more years of army service. Recalling later that some officers had come to the school armed with copies of classroom tests given to them by friends who had attended the school the previous year, he noted, "I knew I would have to study harder than I ever dreamed of studying before in my life."[3]

He was motivated in other ways as well. When his classmates debated who would be the best student, and who would qualify for the class of twenty-four to stay another year and attend the War College, the more prestigious service school that was a prerequisite for army leadership at the highest levels, no one named him. He felt even more pressure when he became eligible to take an exam for promotion to first lieutenant in December 1906. At age twenty-five, with a wife and mother-in-law now residing with him in the comparatively luxurious style they expected, he desperately needed the extra pay, and he wanted the first lieutenant's silver bar as validation that he was succeeding in his chosen profession. When it came on March 7, 1907, little more than three months after he had passed the promotion exam, he saw it as affirmation of his fitness.

Ranked first in his class and therefore certain of a second year at Fort Leavenworth, he was among five students General Bell chose to help train National Guard units in the summer of 1907. His assignment was Pennsylvania's Thirteenth Regiment. Although he spent only a week training the unit, regimental Colonel F. W. Stillwell was so impressed by Marshall's teaching and motivational ability that he invited him back for the next summer.

As an instructor, and with Lily's companionship, Marshall enjoyed the social side of army life, while with the other officers he plunged into such masculine diversions as hunting and riding. Among those on garrison duty at Leavenworth was First Lieutenant Douglas MacArthur. Not surprisingly, as MacArthur biographer William Manchester has noted, Marshall and MacArthur "rubbed each other the wrong way."[4] Where MacArthur was the confident egotist, Marshall was the humble servant-leader, eager to get ahead in the army but willing to subordinate himself for the greater good of the service. As a son of the celebrated and beloved Lieutenant General Arthur MacArthur, commander of U.S. forces in the Philippines and a Medal of Honor recipient, Douglas MacArthur felt that he had much to prove, and didn't hesitate to elbow others aside in order to prove it. Marshall, whose reserve came naturally, did his best to keep his distance from MacArthur.

On the morning of September 21, 1909, Marshall received a telephone call giving him the bad news that his father had suffered a stroke. He set off for Uniontown immediately, but George Sr. died before he got there. Burial was in the Bradford family plot in Allegheny, across the river from Pittsburgh, with full Masonic ritual. To assure Mrs. Marshall's financial security, George Jr., his sister Marie, and his older brother Stuart assigned her their inheritances. The widow spent the rest of her life dividing her time between Uniontown and, from October to Easter, the Haddon Hall Hotel in Atlantic City, New Jersey—at the time a pleasant and popular seaside resort—where she received regular visits from her children.

╬══╬

In the late summer of 1910, after the last of his four years as an instructor at Fort Leavenworth ended, Marshall took two months of accumulated leave, and an additional three in which he would be on half-salary, to take Lily on a grand tour of Europe. In their first opportunity since their marriage for a genuine honeymoon, they spent a month in England, two weeks in Paris, a month in the French chateau country, and five weeks in Florence and Rome, and then went on to Austria. On January 9, 1911, they took slow—and relatively inexpensive—passage from Trieste bound for home. Marshall was quite proud of having covered six countries "on a shoestring."[5]

Back in the States, at the end of January, Marshall assumed command of Company D, Twenty-fourth Infantry, at Madison Barracks, Sackets Harbor, New York, on the shores of Lake Ontario. After three months, friends in the War Department provided welcome relief from the frigid climate by arranging his transfer to Washington, D.C., in 1912 to assist in the planning of a large peacetime maneuver. Involving 17,000 men and elements of three divisions along the U.S.-Mexican border, the maneuver was intended to serve not only as a training exercise, but also a warning to the revolutionary government of Porforio Díaz to respect the Texas border in its pursuit of rebels.

Marshall proved to be a brilliant staff officer and was given much credit, not only by his superiors, but in the popular press, for making the maneuvers a success. Still, he longed for field service, actively leading troops, not sitting behind a Washington desk. In August 1913, he welcomed new orders to return to the Philippines, where he would get more of the field experience he craved. This time he would be accompanied by Lily, who planned to spend the three hottest months traveling in Japan.

On August 5, Marshall reported to the Thirteenth Infantry at Fort McKinley near Manila and quickly realized that no first lieutenant there surpassed his training and experience. Certainly, no West Point junior officer could match his record. He had planned maneuvers involving 17,000 men!

Yet, eleven years after his commissioning in the Regular Army and a decade after he had first arrived in the Philippines to help suppress *insurrectos,* he was still a first lieutenant. Blocked from further promotion by officers who had gotten their commissions in the Spanish-American War—these combat veterans were given preferential treatment—he noted with some chagrin that his own commanding officer, Captain E. J. Williams, had even been his student at Fort Leavenworth.

After several months of commanding one hundred men in M Company, Marshall received orders to serve as adjutant on the staff of the "White Force" in large maneuvers to test the readiness of the Philippine defenses. Motivated by War Department concerns that the Japanese might decide that their triumph in the recent Russo-Japanese War (1904–1905) left them free to seek general domination of the Pacific, the Philippine Department, commanded by former army chief of staff J. Franklin Bell, laid out a simulation exercise in which the White Force would launch an amphibious assault against the defending Brown Force, with the objective of taking Manila. When it became obvious to his immediate subordinates, including Marshall, that the courtly colonel whom Bell had assigned to command the White Force not only had a penchant for strong drink, but lacked the required field command ability, and that his second in command was also inadequate, Marshall recommended to Bell's staff that both the colonel and his number two be retained in nominal command while he served as the actual commander. It was a bold, even impertinent suggestion, but Bell accepted it, and thus George Marshall, a mere first lieutenant, came to command the largest field force in the Philippines in a high-stakes military war game.

With nearly 5,000 men in White Force, Marshall was opposed by two full colonels in the Brown Force, who had all the advantages of rank in obtaining supplies and equipment. When the mock invasion commenced on January 22, 1914, the White attackers were to depart from ports in Luzon, debark at Batangas, and go ashore in small boats. But a shortage of craft delayed the assault until January 29. These complications forced Marshall to improvise, and a young West Point first lieutenant leading a White Force infantry company observed the improvisations with amazement. He watched Marshall in the shade of a clump of bamboo trees with a map spread before him dictate with perfect self-assurance an order to attack to break through the enemy line.

The company commander was Henry H. Arnold, whose genial nature at West Point had earned him the enduring nickname "Hap." He would go on, in World War II, to command the Eighth Air Force and to become one of the key architects of the U.S. Air Force after the war. For now, he stood in awe of Marshall, whose plan, he later recalled, brought White Force a resounding victory.

"When I returned from the maneuvers," Arnold later recalled, "I told my wife I had met a man who was going to be the chief of staff of the army some day."[6]

With his men having convincingly defeated the other side, and showered with praise for assuming a difficult task that he carried out successfully, Marshall suddenly found himself the subject of stories that swept through the officer ranks of the Manila garrison. Word buzzed about that General Bell had called Marshall the greatest military genius since Stonewall Jackson. In his assessment, Marshall's official biographer, Dr. Forrest C. Pogue, endeavored to separate fact from legend. "The achievement demonstrated the development of a fine staff officer," Pogue wrote, and "the extra glamour of the demonstration gave a dazzle to Marshall's name that helped in the future to make sure that his associates and superiors did not forget him."[7]

The maneuvers did take their toll on Marshall, however. Exhausted, he was granted two months of sick leave that were extended by another two months' regular leave. Marshall and Lily used them to travel in Japan, Manchuria, and Korea. It was not all pleasure. Marshall spent a good deal of time studying Russo-Japanese War battlefields and talking with Japanese officers, who invited him to witness troop exercises, including night attacks. On his return to Manila, Marshall settled into routines of garrison duty during the week and a social life of weekend dances and wives' teas punctuated by recreational horseback rides and hikes.

When Brigadier General Hunter Liggett, a former student of Marshall's at Leavenworth and an associate in maneuvers in Connecticut, arrived to command the Provisional Infantry Brigade at Fort McKinley in March 1915, one of his first acts was to make Marshall his aide. Less than a year later, Liggett took over from J. Franklin Bell and carried Marshall along with him. Although he was now aide de camp to the most senior officer in the Philippines, Marshall was still a first lieutenant at the age of thirty-five. Intensely frustrated by the stagnation in promotion in the infantry, he wrote to General

E. W. Nichols, superintendent of the Virginia Military Institute, that he was making tentative plans to resign his commission. With prospects for advancement so restricted by law and by the accumulation of large numbers of men of nearly the same age all in a single grade, he said, he did not feel it was right to waste his best years in a vain struggle against insurmountable difficulties.

Weighing the temptation to accept an absolutely assured and fairly soft living, albeit with little or no prospect of advancement, against the difficulties and dangers of starting anew in civilian life at his age, Marshall confessed to Nichols his feeling that, with only one life, to passively accept his present secured position would mean that he lacked the backbone and necessary moral courage to do the right thing. Nichols answered thoughtfully: "I would advise you to stick to it. If you do, I am sure in time you will be among the high ranking officers in the service."[8] America's entry into the Great War, "the European War," would go a long way to proving Nichols's prediction prescient.

CHAPTER 3

This Little Village

WHILE MARSHALL FRETTED OVER THE U.S. ARMY'S GLACIAL PACE IN promoting its junior officers, nations in Europe that were never slow to find a reason to go to war suddenly rushed to arms in the summer of 1914. The government of Austria-Hungary used the Serbian-backed assassination of Archduke Franz (or Francis) Ferdinand, the aging heir to the throne of its "dual monarchy," in June 1914 as an excuse to punish Serbia and thereby discourage the anti-imperial nationalist movement that was developing in the Balkans. Instead of the limited war Austria-Hungary wanted, the great powers of Europe, bound to the lesser powers and to one another by a web of public treaties and secret agreements, commenced a conflict that came to be known as the "Great War," which enveloped the continent and extended to Europe's colonies in Africa and the Near and Far East.

The United States, under the leadership of the scholarly and apparently pacifist President Woodrow Wilson, proclaimed absolute neutrality in what most Americans referred to as the "European War." Even in the face of German provocations—with atrocity stories hyped by British propagandists and actual violations of U.S. neutrality on the high seas, culminating in the 1915 U-boat attack on the British ocean liner *Lusitania,* in which 1,198 passengers and crew, including 128 Americans, died—Wilson resisted calls by Theodore Roosevelt and others for entry into the war.

From Marshall's perspective in the Philippines, Japanese expansionism loomed as a more likely future threat to U.S. interests than did any European war. For the present, however, Marshall believed that the deteriorating relations between the United States and its neighbor Mexico presented a threat more pressing than either the situation in Europe or the likely future situation in the Philippines. Moreover, whereas Wilson was reluctant to prepare an army to fight in Europe, he demonstrated his eagerness to dispatch troops to the Mexican border, and Marshall was keenly intensely frustrated by his posting so far from the imminent action.

Roused to ire by a lethal raid the Mexican revolutionary "bandit" Pancho Villa led into Columbus, New Mexico, on March 9, 1916, that killed seventeen Americans, the president sent some 11,000 troops under Major General John J. Pershing on a "Punitive Expedition" to pursue and capture or kill Villa and his army of *villistas.* When it became clear that the resources of the Regular Army were insufficient to carry on both the expeditionary and defensive phases of the mission, President Wilson federalized the National Guard in the border states, and Congress passed the National Defense Act of 1916, which created a Reserve Officers' Training Corps (ROTC) and several training camps with three-month courses designed to mass-produce second lieutenants (who were soon mocked as "ninety-day-wonders").

Here at last was an opportunity for advancement. Eager to join the fray on the border, Marshall hoped that his mentor, General J. Franklin Bell, would be transferred from the Philippines to Mexico and take him along. Instead, however, Bell was assigned to the placid Presidio in San Francisco as commander of the Western Department. Marshall did go along—not to Mexico, but to the city by the Golden Gate as Bell's aide. His disappointment at not going to war in command of troops was assuaged by an order to appear at Fort McDowell before a promotion board, which unanimously recommended his elevation to captain, effective August 14, 1916.

Although he had been denied the opportunity to enhance his service record by participating in the pursuit of Villa, Marshall discovered that his performance in maneuvers had made him sufficiently famous to prompt the men serving under him in a newly created Officers Reserve Corps thirty-day training camp at Monterey, California, to bestow on him the sobriquet of "Dynamite." A further boost to his reputation came from Lieutenant Colonel Johnson Hagood, who, in his efficiency report on Marshall's service as his adjutant at a second month-long training camp, conducted at Fort Douglas, Utah, called him a "military genius." To a question as to whether Hagood would like to have Marshall under his command again, Hagood wrote, "This officer is well qualified to command a division, with the rank of major general, in time of war and I would like very much to serve under his command." In the report, dated December 31, 1916, Marshall's thirty-sixth birthday, Hagood proposed that Marshall be jumped in rank to brigadier general in the Regular Army. Hagood added: "every day this is postponed is a loss to the Army and nation."[1]

✦

Four months after Hagood's glowing endorsement, Marshall was still a captain and still serving as Bell's aide. But a profound change *had* taken place. Marshall was no longer at the Presidio as Bell's aide or conducting thirty-day training stints in Monterey and Fort Douglas, but was in the shipping office on Governors Island in New York Harbor, awaiting orders to depart for France with the American Expeditionary Force (AEF). On April 6, 1917, at the request of Woodrow Wilson—elected to a second term in November 1916 largely on his campaign slogan, "He Kept Us Out of War"—Congress declared war on Germany and the other Central Powers (Austria-Hungary and Turkey).

Itching to leave for France with the first contingent of troops under Pershing, Captain Marshall called upon a long list of army friends garnered over fourteen years to help him. Major General William L. Sibert, chosen to head the army's first combat division, recalled Marshall's outstanding work at the Monterey training camp and asked Bell to release him. Bell sent Marshall to meet Sibert at Bowling Green, on the tip of Lower Manhattan, in full view of the Statue of Liberty. There Sibert told him that he would be sailing to France in thirty-six hours.

Marshall rushed to pack his wife, Lily, off to Lexington, Virginia, where she would live for the duration of his war service. Next, on June 10, 1917, he reported to Hoboken, New Jersey, and what had been the North German Lloyd Line docks, now commandeered by the U.S. government.

As the men of the U.S. First Division left trains in the Hoboken meadows and marched toward the docks and the troop transports that had been converted from cargo ships plying the South and Central American fruit trade, Captain Marshall stood at a window of the shipping office with the port commander. Watching a seemingly endless column of infantry pass by on a cold and drizzling morning and boarding in almost total silence, he remarked, "The men seem very solemn."

"Of course they are," said the official in a grimly dramatic tone. "We are watching the harvest of death."[2]

A tableau that to Marshall was historic quickly turned both comic and alarming as the impressive armada was forced to halt in the harbor because no one on shore had remembered to remove an antisubmarine chain that blocked the channel. Marshall was even more shocked to learn that no one boarding the ships had been issued ammunition. It suddenly dawned on him that the U.S. Army was hardly prepared to fight a world war.

Attended by an escort of six destroyers, the first U.S. troop convoy steamed across Atlantic waters that were rumored to be stalked by German U-boats. Only one false alarm relived the tedium of the long voyage, however, and Marshall, following General William Sibert, was the second man ashore at St. Nazaire on June 26, 1917. He was eager to get into the action at long last but he also felt a keen sympathy for the French, who had suffered through three years of war marked by appalling casualty counts. The small number of French women, children, and the few men who watched the First Division debark showed no enthusiasm over the arrival of Americans. If any of the weary people of St. Nazaire expected them to rush into battle, they soon learned that General John J. "Black Jack" Pershing, commander of the American Expeditionary Force, was in no hurry to do so. Because the First Division was an entirely new organization filled with green recruits, Pershing was not about to toss them piecemeal into combat only to be killed. Marshall agreed that it was essential that the men be disciplined and the organization well trained before entering the line, especially because a reverse, however small, suffered by the first American unit committed to the battle would have a depressing effect on all of the Allies, encourage the enemy, and give politicians in the United States an opportunity to make mischief with the army.[3]

French and British officers, who had been fighting the Germans for three years, eyed the Americans skeptically—these troops whose leaders had boasted that once the Yanks were "over there" the war would soon end—as they settled into a training ground in Lorraine. When a battalion was sent to Paris to march down the Champs-Elysées on Bastille Day (July 14), Marshall met a brash and self-confident cavalryman, Captain George S. Patton Jr., who was commander of Pershing's headquarters. The two captains watched the Americans and the French marching, and remarked to one another that the U.S. doughboys looked shabby and unsoldierly in comparison to the French. They agreed that this would have to change, and quickly.

The next day, Marshall accompanied General Sibert to the site chosen as his headquarters in Gondrecourt. They were greeted there by the son and namesake of President Theodore Roosevelt. Ted (as he was familiarly called) and two of his brothers, Archie and Quentin, made their father proud by volunteering immediately after the declaration of war (April 6, 1917). Quentin Roosevelt, the youngest, was a dashing fighter pilot. A fourth son, Kermit, had enlisted in the British army before the U.S. declaration and was serving in Mesopotamia; he would eventually transfer to the U.S. Army and join his brothers in France.

The captain was billeted in the house of a middle-aged couple, Madame Jouette and her husband, whom Marshall described in his memoir as a wizened little fellow who looked like a scoundrel—and (as far as Marshall was concerned) soon proved to be one, passing much of his time in surreptitious visits to his mistress across the street. Marshall would live with the Jouettes for six months, a tough period consumed mostly in training, which he and other American officers described as the "Winter of Valley Forge." Marshall credited Madame Jouette's kindness and enthusiasm with helping him to "keep a stiff upper lip and wear an optimistic smile those days."[4]

For the first several weeks of his assignment in France, Marshall traveled more than a hundred miles a day, inspecting sites for training troops, arranging for the construction of barracks and bathhouses, and explaining to French officials how the U.S. Army was organized and assuring them that the doughboys would fight, but only when Pershing decided they were ready. He also explained that the people of the United States and their general would allow their citizen soldiers to go into battle only with American commanders and only under the Stars and Stripes, not as adjuncts to the French or British armies.

Having nearly quit the army in frustration at spending nine years as a first lieutenant, Marshall was now caught up in the greatly accelerated wartime pace of promotion. In August 1917, less than thirteen months after he made captain, he was given the temporary rank of major, although, even then, he was already doing a job customarily performed by a lieutenant colonel. That same month, he was an observer with other American officers of a French attack along the Verdun front. From a hilltop he watched what he described as the first and last "picture book battle" he would see, combat in which one great military formation fought another. By and large, the war on the Western Front was a trench-to-trench slaughter, characterized more by bloody stalemate and attrition than bold maneuver.

During the dismal, wet, cold, and dispiriting autumn of 1917, several encounters with Pershing brought Marshall close to jeopardizing what was now clearly a very promising future in the army. The first episode involved a review of troops that Pershing deemed unsatisfactory because there were too few men and not enough time to review them. Turning to Marshall, Pershing angrily demanded, "What is this?" After hearing Marshall's explanation that he had done his best with the units he had and that he had followed instructions from the secretary of the General Staff, Pershing departed in an evil humor. He returned a few days later, on short notice, to observe an exercise in trench warfare developed by Major Ted Roosevelt. Marshall gave General Sibert a heads-up, but Sibert nevertheless failed to greet Pershing when the American Expeditionary Force (AEF) arrived by train in the morning. Marshall not only found himself at a loss to explain Sibert's absence to Pershing, but he also had to endure the wrath of Sibert, who upbraided him for having gotten to the train ahead of him. With Pershing in a sour mood, the men in place and ready in trenches the French had prepared—and with Roosevelt eager to lead the mock attack—the AEF chief and his retinue of aides assembled to watch.

"There was a lot of shooting," Marshall wrote in his memoir, "and a lot of dashing around from trench to trench and a lot of grenade throwing and general hullabaloo, and then it was all over."

"Assemble the officers," Pershing ordered. After such an exercise, the commanding officer (in this case Sibert) was expected to deliver a critique. Aware that Sibert had not been informed of the details of Roosevelt's exercise, and knowing that Pershing had made no secret of his low esteem for William Sibert, Marshall watched with anxious sympathy as Pershing turned expectantly to his commanding officer. Sure enough, Sibert was unable to provide a satisfactory critique. This provoked a severe dressing-down from General Pershing in front of all the officers. After the AEF chief went on to disparage the performance of the entire division, Major Marshall made bold to intervene. Approaching Pershing, by all accounts a most intimidating figure, Marshall proceeded to defend everything Pershing had faulted.

Pershing shrugged and turned away. Incredibly, Marshall gripped the general's arm and exclaimed, "General Pershing, there's something to be said here, and I think I should say it because I've been here longest."

Pershing wheeled about angrily and demanded, "What have you got to say?"

For the next few minutes the West Point alumnus who was twenty years older, had fought in the Spanish-American War and the Philippines, had been personally promoted by Theodore Roosevelt from captain to brigadier general in one leap, and had led the Punitive Expedition, listened while the VMI major unleashed a torrent of complaints about inadequate supplies, men without proper footwear, insufficient quarters, troops sleeping in barns, lack of transport, and the disdain French officers showed to all Americans.

In reply, Pershing gave the daring youngster a hint of the stress at the top of a chain of command: "Well, you must appreciate the troubles *we* have."

Marshall was unrelenting. "Yes, General," he responded, "but we have them every day and many a day, and we have to solve every one of them by night."

Looking back on the episode, Marshall later explained, "I was just mad all over, I thought I had gotten in it up to my neck—I might as well not try to float but to splash a little bit." At the time, fellow officers told him he was sunk. He was a fool. His army career was over. "All I can see is that I may get troop duty instead of staff duty, and certainly that would be a great success," Marshall told them.[5]

Whether General Pershing tacitly approved of Marshall's blunt initiative or he was just too busy to declare a case of insubordination, Marshall suffered no retribution for his frank outburst, which, if anything, added to the formidable legend that continued to grow about him. His status unchanged, he went on with his work as operations officer, arranging transport and other details for the First Division's move from the Gondrecourt training area to the Einville sector some twenty miles to the east. The scene of very heavy fighting in August 1914, the area of the front was so quiet in October 1917 that at one point where a small village lay partly within the German line on the edge of the no-man's-land between the two opposing forces the villagers walked about as if there were no war. The wide front over which the Americans were distributed required Marshall to travel long distances to battalions starting at dawn and ending at dusk. For him, the first thrill of service in the trenches soon passed with a realization of the mud and other discomforts as well as the dearth of excitement in so quiet and dreary a sector.

As Marshall was about to leave by automobile to visit the Second Battalion, Sixteenth Infantry, on the morning of November 3, the French commander, General Paul Emile Bordeaux, rushed from his office and excitedly exclaimed in French that the first American soldiers had been killed early that morning by intense German artillery fire. Worse, Company F, Sixteenth Infantry, had cut a hole in the barbed wire in front of their trenches, which allowed a German raiding party to rush through, capture twelve men, and kill three. Of these, one was shot in the head, the second clubbed to death, and the third had his throat slit.

Viewing the gruesome scene with the French general, Marshall listened as Bordeaux drew the conclusion that the Americans had not made a sufficiently determined resistance. Bristling at the slur, Marshall retorted that Bordeaux need entertain no fears regarding the fighting skill of the American soldier. He then opined that General Pershing would be much concerned when he learned of the Frenchman's remarks. Evidently eager to make amends for the slight to the valor of the slain men, and to keep Pershing out of it, Bordeaux ordered them buried with elaborate military honors. Lauding the men he referred to as a humble corporal and two private soldiers, and citing their deaths as instances of extraordinary valor, Bordeaux pledged to inscribe on their tomb, "Here lie the first soldiers of the famous Republic of the United States to fall on the soil of France, for justice and liberty." Marshall was so moved by the remarks that he asked Bordeaux to dictate them to his French aide so that he could include them in his report to the First Division commander.

Four weeks after this, Marshall learned that the general who had remembered him from their days at a training camp in Monterey, California, and brought him to war in France, had been ordered home by the War Department. Determined to get rid of Sibert, General Pershing had recommended that he be named head of a Chemical Warfare Service that Pershing proposed be created, even though General Sibert was commissioned in the Engineers. His replacement was General Robert Lee Bullard, who had been the commander of the First Division's Second Brigade. Marshall knew him slightly; Bullard had complimented him for a brief period of work as acting division chief of staff. Because almost all the officers at the division headquarters had been his close friends or students at Leavenworth, Marshall felt free to express his bitterness about Sibert's removal. What his friends at GHQ (general headquarters) did not tell him as he ranted was that he was in line to be named Bullard's chief of staff until, informed of these outbursts of ill temper, Bullard decided that Marshall had no business being made chief of staff in that state of mind. Marshall said later that he realized he had made a mistake, that his failure to restrain his temper had kept him from quickly becoming brigadier general. "This was the lesson that I got right there," he said, "and I never forgot it."[6]

He was nevertheless promoted to lieutenant colonel in the wartime National Army during Christmas 1917. Marshall continued visiting troops at the front and developed a strong sympathy for the infantryman, who had to march tremendous distances, live in mud, go long periods without a full meal, and fight in places he'd never seen before. To celebrate December 25 and his new rank, Marshall invited his French aide, three officer friends, and a French interpreter to Madame Jouette's snug house for a Christmas dinner.

A week later, as operations officer, Marshall organized the movement of the First Division to a sector midway between St. Mihiel and the Moselle

River in northeastern France to relieve the French Moroccan Division. He observed how these colonial troops, men of the rough soldier-of-fortune type, greeted the fresh-faced Americans with the casual tolerance of war-worn veterans. Departing, they warned them that they would most likely be serving in dilapidated trenches and dugouts, usually filled with water and mud.

Barely settled into the new sector, the First Division was visited by generals sent from training camps in the United States to inspect conditions in France. Marshall resented the burden of having to escort these visitors and explain the division's organization, but was amused to learn in the midst of his deep winter labors how the home front had blossomed into great cantonments and how Selective Service was conducting successive drafts, swelling the U.S. Army's ranks to levels not seen since the Civil War. He heard tales of instruction in singing and boxing, of consultation with psychiatric experts, and of many other strange additions to army life.

On March 1, 1918, after a German mortar barrage and an attack on the First Division's front by a section of *Flammenwerfer* (flamethrower) troops, the Americans had what Marshall termed their first nearby encounter with Germans. Elements of the First Division launched a counterattack across snowy ground, and, the next morning, Premier Georges Clemenceau arrived at the front to show the gratitude of France by awarding the men in the unit the Croix de Guerre as a light snow fell. One soldier who had missed the ceremony ran after Clemenceau and apologized for being late. Pinning the medal on him, Clemenceau said, "That does not matter, for you were not late yesterday."

That the head of the French government would travel from Paris and tramp through mud to award medals to a handful of men in a war in which daily death tolls ran into the thousands signified the desire of the French government to demonstrate its appreciation that Americans had joined in the battle, even if it was only to a limited extent at that time. At the same time, the French military high command waited in frustration for Pershing to commit the full weight of U.S. troops that had been streaming across the Atlantic in increasing quantities for nine months. Despite Allied pleas for AEF troops to move to the front and join the fight, Pershing insisted that the bulk of his men were not ready for battle. As the snow disappeared from no-man's-land and the bottoms of trenches became even muddier, tensions heightened in the war councils of Paris and London in anticipation of a German spring offensive. Pershing had allowed only the First Division to move forward. Its limited raids were recorded in scrupulous detail so that they could be studied by other units in training.

+⇒=+

Determined to strike a decisive blow before Pershing unleashed his troops, the Germans commenced the first of the so-called Ludendorff Offensives. Code named "Michael," the St. Quentin Offensive stepped off on March 21, 1918, with the objective of driving between the British and the French lines, then sweeping through to Paris. As General Philippe Pétain withdrew the First French Army back to defend the capital, Pershing recognized a calamity in the making and offered Pétain all of his divisions for use wherever Pétain needed them.

"In this critical situation General Pershing rose to greatness," Marshall wrote in his memoir. "Surrendering the direct control of his own troops, which he had so vigorously maintained in the face of repeated endeavors to prevent the formation of an American army, he released them to be scattered over four hundred miles of front. Temporarily jeopardizing his own men and even American prestige, he laid all his cards on the table and directed every move toward the salvage of the Allied wreck."[7]

Pétain requested that the First Division be moved from Lorraine to the front in Picardy. After three days of marching, the headquarters of the First Division paused two days at a small village to make a reconnaissance of the front assigned to the division. Faced with the German offensive, the Allies were compelled to submerge their mutual distrust and establish a unified command under sixty-seven-year-old Marshal Ferdinand Foch (Pétain's superior), with Pershing reserving the right to form an exclusively American army once the front stabilized. Far below the pay grades of the French field marshal and the American general, operations officer George C. Marshall settled into the post of command of the U.S. First Division in the wine cellar of a small chateau at Le Mesnil-Saint-Firmin.

As yet unscarred by the trenches and broad muddy fields that marked the no-man's-land the division had left behind, the Picardy countryside presented fields bearing promising crops, long stretches of level land broken by gentle hill slopes, and good roads. In a war that introduced the airplane, some of the fields suddenly blossomed with small tents to house pilots and mechanics and bigger ones to serve as hangars. Exhibiting admiration for this new breed of warrior, Marshall wrote that it was interesting to ride through these camps where the combat planes were continually arriving or departing "with many spectacular loops and other dangerous gyrations." Among the aviators made celebrities at home by American war correspondents were captains Eddie Rickenbaker and Billy Mitchell and Lieutenant Quentin Roosevelt, whose place in the sky made news because his father was the former president. As an operations officer planning infantry actions, Marshall relied on reports by such daring aviators as these, as well as from humbler men in observation balloons positioned with views of the front. Yet none of this fully substituted for the daily visits he made to the men in the lines. When traveling by car was impossible or excessively dangerous because of German artillery fire, Marshall mounted a horse.

On May 16, 1918, Marshall climbed into a saddle and set out from Division GHQ on an inspection tour before the reinforced Twenty-eighth Infantry Regiment launched an attack to take the crossroads village of Cantigny, near Montdidier in the Somme region. About 4,000 U.S. troops would be assisted by French tanks. Marshall was acutely interested in the operation, for which he had done most of the planning, down to each man's part in it. Under his supervision, the regiment had spent a week rehearsing in a rear area before returning to the front. In a hurry to get going on his inspection, he nudged the horse into a lope before adjusting himself in the saddle or straightening the reins. The horse slipped, went down, and rolled over twice, with Marshall's left foot in the stirrup. His ankle fractured, but he remounted and returned to headquarters. Unable to sleep well because of the pain, he continued to work day and night sitting up, his ankle tightly taped and his foot resting on a table or chair.

On the night of May 27, war correspondents assembled at headquarters. Because Marshall had been bombarded with complaints about excessive secrecy regarding action plans, he gave the newsmen a complete briefing. When James Hopper of *Collier's* magazine, who had gained fame for his eyewitness reporting of the 1906 San Francisco earthquake, inquired if there were restrictions on where they could go, Marshall said the only prohibition General Bullard had placed on their movement was that they should not precede the first infantry wave into Cantigny.

As the morning of May 28 dawned clear and the preliminary artillery barrage began, the village took on the appearance of an active volcano. At 6:45 A.M., the infantry moved out in perfect alignment. Reports of progress came into division HQ every five minutes by telephone. Marshall noted that the success of this phase of the operation was so complete and the list of casualties so small that everyone was filled with enthusiasm and delight. Entering Cantigny just behind the first wave of infantry, James Hopper suddenly found himself perplexed and embarrassed when a group of Germans surrendered to *him*.

⊢⇒⇒⊣

Marshall was thrilled at the success of the Cantigny operation—the first major American action of the war—but he was even more aware of what the price of failure would have been. He called such a prospect "unthinkable." It would have depressed the morale of the entire army, not to mention that of the Allies generally. The casualty toll had been heavy, but its severity had only gone to demonstrate conclusively the fighting qualities, commitment, and fortitude of the American soldier.

Marshall never lost focus on the individual soldier, but he also had a genius for taking in and holding on to the big picture. To him, Cantigny was a splendid achievement of American arms as well as a closing of the circle of American history. He recognized that, having left Europe 300 years earlier to "escape oppression and the loss of personal liberties," the descendents of America's first settlers returned to the Old Country to launch, on May 29, 1918, "their first attack on the remaining forces of autocracy" to secure for the people of Europe the same liberty and justice they enjoyed in the United States.[8] At the time of this realization, Marshall could not have known that his role in the AEF campaign following Cantigny would be very different from what he'd hoped for, yet much greater than he had imagined.

CHAPTER 4

The Wizard

ON JUNE 18, 1918, LIEUTENANT COLONEL GEORGE C. MARSHALL started a letter up the AEF chain of command asking to be put in charge of troops. He certainly could not complain about his rapid promotion, but he did point out that he had been on staff duty since February 1915 and claimed he was tired from the strain of office work. First Division commander General Robert Lee Bullard passed on the request without endorsement, but cited Marshall's special fitness for staff work. This was by no means a slight. Staff officers, who occupy a level between the high commanders who make the plans and the field commanders who execute them, are essential to large modern armies—though it is true that staff officers rarely have the opportunity to earn the kind of distinction that gets them to the very top. Marshall's brilliance as a staff officer was recognized and rewarded, but always within the context of staff assignments. His June 18 letter resulted in his being ordered to General Pershing's headquarters at Chaumont in July. His immediate boss was to be the AEF's chief of operations, Colonel Fox Connor.

In his memoirs, Marshall lamented his failure to obtain a transfer to a field command and bemoaned the irony that his request for frontline combat duty got him assigned instead to headquarters, far from the front. The characteristically stoic Marshall had a difficult time controlling his emotions as he bade farewell to the men of the First Division. He had, however, advanced from division-level staff work, with its daily problems of feeding, clothing, and training soldiers, to staff work at the army level. The issues with which he now wrestled were ocean tonnage, ports of debarkation, and training divisions newly arrived from the United States. In addition to logistics, Marshall was to participate in planning major operations. It was, as he later recalled, all "a different world from that in which I had lived during the past year."[1]

Colonel Connor wasted no time putting Marshall to work. The morning after Marshall arrived, Connor ordered him to gather all possible information regarding the St. Mihiel salient and to work on a plan to push it back—in military parlance, to "reduce" it. A V-shaped bulge of the German line stabbing deeply into the Allied front, the salient was approximately thirty-five miles wide at its base and had been formed near the very beginning of the war, in September 1914, as part of the German attempt to take the French fortress of Verdun. Ever since then, it had posed a strategic threat to the Allies. Just how and when the salient was to be attacked by Pershing's all-American First Army would become a matter of heated debate between Pershing and France's Marshal Ferdinand Foch. Eager to exploit a German retreat after an Allied victory at the Second Battle of the Marne (July 15–18), Foch proposed that Pershing switch two divisions from the St. Mihiel assault to reinforce the French Second Army for a combined attack north of the Marne. Pershing replied angrily, "This virtually destroys the American army that we have been trying so long to form."

Foch answered in the same testy mood, "Voulez-vous aller à la bataille?" ("Do you want a part in the battle?")

"Most assuredly," Pershing retorted, "but as an American army and in no other way."[2]

On September 3, 1918, Foch relented for the first time since the end of July. Pershing would attack the St. Mihiel salient with his army intact, but he agreed that as soon as the battle was over, his troops would take over a twenty-mile sector along the Meuse River and the Argonne Forest to prepare for an attack in the direction of the strategic city of Sedan. While the two commanders were sparring, Marshall was promoted to colonel on August 27, and, three days later he saw Foch arrive for the conference with General Pershing that resulted in the compromise. This was Marshall's signal to proceed full speed ahead on planning the St. Mihiel operation. Connor partnered him with Colonel Walter S. Grant, and the two found themselves leading a brand-new staff of a brand-new army, three times the army's normal size, which was just entering the line for the first time and approaching its first independent operation. As if this challenge were not formidable enough, the agreement between Pershing and Foch meant that Marshall, Grant, and the rest of the staff would have to turn on a dime to coordinate preparations for the much larger Meuse-Argonne operation slated to follow the reduction of the St. Mihiel salient.

What the Allies did not know was that the Germans had given up on holding the salient. Consequently, when the Americans attacked a front that the Germans had actually been planning to evacuate, resistance was half-hearted. Within the salient lay a defensive maze of concrete pillboxes connected by trenches, bombproof tunnels, and layers of coiled barbed wire obstacles. Launched against them after a brief artillery barrage in driving rain on September 12 were largely untested Americans and a newly organized tank corps led by Colonel George S. Patton Jr.

At H-hour on D-day (the first-ever use of these designations for the hour and day of attack), impatient American infantrymen chose not to wait for engineers to clear coiled barbed wire barriers, instead trampling over and through them in an attack that caught the enemy by surprise. Outnumbered and slightly out of position, the German force collapsed. In thirty-six hours the Americans took over 13,000 prisoners and captured 466 guns. The Germans lost 5,000 killed and wounded, while the Americans had suffered 7,000 killed and wounded.

+≈≈≈+

Now came an even greater challenge for Marshall. He would have to shift 600,000 men and 900,000 tons of supplies and ammunition from St. Mihiel to the Meuse-Argonne sector some sixty miles forward. Once the success of the St. Mihiel battle seemed assured on the afternoon of the first day (September 12), he turned his attention to executing what was the largest logistical problem of the war. Long convoys of trucks and horse-drawn wagons, buses, trains, and tens of thousands of men on foot had to be moved (and moved secretly) along grossly inadequate, narrow roads and lanes under cover of night. Both Foch and Pershing doubted that this could be done.

In an upstairs office in the town hall of Souilly that had been French headquarters in the fight for Verdun in 1916, Marshall used a telephone to issue the orders, assisted by Colonel Walter Grant and a French officer. Army reserve divisions were started for the new front and the heavy artillery was withdrawn from the St. Mihiel battle and headed west, then turned northward around the tip of the former salient. At the same time, the bulk of the troops and guns had to be withdrawn from the south face of the salient, moved westward and turned north into the zone of the Second French Army. Trucks and buses could make their journey in a night, whereas the horse-drawn transport needed three to six days. Coordination of the movement of trucks, tractors, the animal-drawn vehicles, and foot troops at night over congested roads was complicated by the bilingual nature of the enterprise. It was bad enough that two Americans could stir up a violent argument in a traffic jam, Marshall noted; the addition of a Frenchman to the mix made it highly explosive.

Venturing out from his control post to inspect a fifty-mile stretch of road at night, Marshall found a continuous chain of marching men, horse-drawn vehicles, and, most of all, motor transport. He marveled that in the darkness there were few collisions, although the roadside was littered with broken-down cars, trucks, and motorcycles. A truck hauling a protruding, long steel central beam for a canvas airplane hangar had sideswiped two mules pulling machine guns, injuring both animals. A bus carrying soldiers had run off a bridge into the Meuse River, and a following truck had swerved and wedged into the bridge. At the same point the next night another busload of soldiers crashed through a railroad crossing gate and was struck by the locomotive of an oncoming train, resulting in several deaths. But mishaps like these were the exception, not the rule.

Nimbly improvising on his troop movement plan as changing conditions dictated, Marshall alternately shouted new orders by landline telephone to officers on the road who could barely hear him over the roar of traffic, or he spoke quietly and patiently to others who barged into his office seeking clarifications or confirmations. On paper and in his head were details of thirty-seven railheads and a hundred villages along the maze of routes, and all with French names that his rudimentary command of the language barely enabled him to pronounce.

By the night of September 24, the transfer of men and supplies was completed. Noting with pride and relief that the entire movement had been carried out without a single element failing to reach its place on the date scheduled, Marshall recorded that everything had been accomplished one day earlier than Foch considered possible. The military correspondent of the *Times* of London, Colonel Charles Repington, exclaimed, "It was a fine piece of Staff work and no other Staff could have done it better." Some awed army wiseacre tagged Marshall with the nickname "Wizard."[3] What was clear to everyone, both above Marshall's rank and below, was the man's genius for logistical management. Born warriors like Napoleon or (as he was already proving himself) George Patton were rare, but natural staff officers were even rarer. Whether by his preferred route or not, George Marshall had found his entrée into the highest ranks of the U.S. Army.

According to the plan Foch and Pershing had devised, the Meuse-Argonne battle was to commence on September 26, 1918, with a Franco-American northeasterly thrust to Sedan, while three other coordinated attacks were launched over a region stretching westward to the English Channel. On September 25, Marshall visited several corps and division headquarters to make certain that various eleventh-hour modifications in troop movements were understood. Instead of leading men in battle as he had hoped to do, he was again the supremely competent staff officer meticulously checking details. He had enrolled at VMI with dreams of glorious combat, but for seventeen years the army in its wisdom had seen him as a teacher, a planner, a brilliant tactician, a peerless logistical manager—in short, the ideal staff officer. In the meantime, some of those he had taught were already generals. Yet, having planned and executed the transfer of an army in the midst of one battle to the site of another without the enemy knowing it, he had accomplished a feat that rivaled George Washington's nighttime withdrawal of his army from Long Island under the noses of the British in 1776, and he had carried out a movement and commitment of troops in combat on a scale that would not be matched by another American until World War II.

Denied the opportunity of personal battle, Marshall received the reports of the start of the execution of the Meuse-Argonne assault plan to which he had made a significant contribution, and he stood ready to alter it whenever and wherever battlefield conditions changed. By nightfall of the first day, it appeared that the Germans had been caught by surprise and that the advance had broken completely through defenses on two portions of the front, but most of the divisions, engaged in their first fight, were not experienced enough to exploit their advantage. A French visitor to Pershing's headquarters observed that the Americans were dying bravely, but were not advancing, or were advancing very little. Writing disdainfully of ever-present visitors—naval, staff, civilian, and foreign—who in a few cases were able to cross the devastated battle zone of the First Army, Marshall recorded that they spread reports all over France and England that the American soldiers had failed and had proven incompetent to coordinate so large an undertaking.

The opening of the Meuse-Argonne offensive was a nightmare of logistics that even left Premier Clemenceau caught in a traffic jam. Blocked by a column of trucks, he was told by drivers that they had been held up for two nights. The unraveling involved columns of vehicles stretching ten or more kilometers (about six miles or more), sometimes in both directions, on roads that had been raked by artillery. At the same time, Marshall was dealing with the demands and exigencies of the battle, including an order for an overnight transfer of an additional 140,000 men another sixty miles or so.

Among reports to headquarters was one that listed hundreds of infantrymen under the command of Major Charles W. Whittlesey who went into the Argonne Forest on the morning of October 18 and were reported as having been "lost." War correspondents seeking to satisfy the American public's appetite for news from the front dubbed them poetically the "Lost Battalion." Actually, two battalions of the 308th Infantry Regiment, this force of 554 men had found themselves cut off from the remainder of the Seventy-Seventh Division and surrounded by a superior number of the enemy. Without food for more than one hundred hours, and harassed continuously by fire from machine guns, rifles, trench mortars, and grenades, they successfully resisted repeated fierce enemy attacks. When one of the wounded was captured he was returned with a written demand for surrender that Whittlesey rejected by simply refusing a reply. When relief finally came on October 7, approximately 194 officers and men were able to walk out of the position they had held. American officers and men killed totaled 107. Whittlesey and four others would receive the Medal of Honor.

+======+

Pershing's AEF consisted of nearly a million soldiers. No American had ever commanded so many. On October 12, 1918, he divided the force, creating the Second Army, commanded by General Robert Lee Bullard. With General Hunter Liggett now heading the First Army, Marshall was moved up to chief of operations. As usual he went to the front frequently. At the end of the month, Foch issued an order for a November drive as far as possible into German-held territory, without attempts at troop alignment as the forces advanced. The units farthest forward were to assist the advance of those that were stalled. As the First Army broke through the lines on the very first day, a reporter at headquarters observed staff officers almost capering before the wall map as pins were moved forward.

Colonel Marshall was not dancing, however. He was worrying over how the rapidity of the advance was making communication between Army HQ and corps and divisions increasingly difficult to manage. In the era before reliable field radio communication, landline telephones were extensively used, but suffered from the inability of Signal Corps personnel to erect poles and lines as fast as the front was now advancing. Carrier pigeons conveying data written on slips of tissue paper were subject to the whims of wind and vicissitudes of shifting units, and sometimes became targets for sharpshooting enemy. Marshall decided that the most reliable alternative was the motorcycle messenger, but even this swift courier was often caught on roads crammed with battle traffic. He worked late into the night to supervise preparation of updated maps to make up for any delay. He would also oversee the drafting of whatever field orders were to be issued to the army the following day. After catching what little sleep he could, he would then return to the office early in the morning to go over the field orders that had been typed during the night, triple-spaced, with four copies. After making any last-minute changes, he handed one of the copies to a mimeographer, and the others were given to officers to dictate by telephone to the distant corps headquarters. Mimeographed copies were handed to motorcyclists for distribution to closer units. Even if the messengers were delayed, at least they carried the very latest maps and orders. In this way, Marshall sought to compensate for inadequate telephone communication and crowded roads by maintaining a steady flow of updated information.

The increasingly frenetic pace of his revisions and communications was a product of the acceleration of events as the war drew to a close. On November 4 and 5, the American advance gained tremendous momentum. The eastern portion of the First Army swung right and came to a halt along the banks of the Meuse. The left wing swept far beyond the Fourth French Army. In the meantime, on the night of November 4, the Rainbow Division passed into and through the area of the Seventy-eighth Division. With the Germans in retreat, the smell of victory was in the air, and with it came a desire among the military leaders of the Allies to crush the enemy forces so completely as to make it impossible for German diplomats to negotiate anything approaching favorable terms for an armistice. Nothing less than total victory would suffice, and nothing but unconditional surrender would be accepted.

As the army that four years earlier had approached within about thirty miles of Paris now reeled back toward Germany under the weight of American and Allied onslaught, the fabric of Kaiser Wilhelm's society rapidly unraveled. War-weary Germans were in a revolutionary mood everywhere. The alliance between Germany and the Central Powers (Austria-Hungary and Turkey) had been defeated on all fronts, leaving the map of Europe to be redrawn by the Allies. From the Dardanelles to the Persian Gulf, the Ottoman Empire was a petroleum-rich corpse waiting to be picked apart by Britain and France.

The war was rushing to its conclusion, and George Marshall, though he had not directly led men in battle, could take great satisfaction in the tactical and logistical roles he had played. But he had one more lesson to learn. It was about the relative weights of strategy, battlefield opportunity, national sentiment, and command authority.

The map posted on Marshall's office wall clearly showed the city of Sedan directly ahead of the advancing American forces. The town was of no great military significance to Pershing's armies, but it was there for the taking, and the AEF was poised to take it. To the French, however, Sedan was of great emotional significance. It was here in 1870 that Emperor Louis Napoleon signed the humiliating treaty with Prussia ending the Franco-Prussian War and yielding to Bismarck and the Kaiser both the coal-rich Alsace and preeminence in Europe's destiny. The town *had* to be liberated by a French army. Foch brushed aside the presence of the U.S. First Army and declared that the city was to be recaptured—and the honor of France reclaimed—by the French Fourth Army.

Pershing understood. But for Marshall, this meant formulating complex operational orders to the First Army to pivot to the left to allow the French, to the rear of the Americans, to move forward. While he labored over this logistical problem at four in the afternoon on November 4, Fox Connor, now a major general and chief of operations of the entire AEF, entered his office and asked him what he was doing. Marshall explained. Connor interrupted. The enemy, he said, was in a critical predicament and should not be given the pause for reorganization that changing the position of the First Army would afford them. The two men fell to discussing the situation for about a half hour, when Connor suddenly declared, "It is General Pershing's desire that the troops of the First Army should capture Sedan, and he directs that orders should be issued accordingly."

Marshall, who understood the importance of Sedan to the French, replied that this was "a rather an important order," and as Connor stood by, he summoned a stenographer and dictated:

1. General Pershing desires that the honor of entering Sedan should fall to the First American Army. He has every confidence that the troops of the First Corps, assisted on their right by the Fifth Corps, will enable him to realize this desire.

2. In transmitting the foregoing message, your attention is invited to the favorable opportunity now existing for pressing our advantage throughout the night.

Connor approved the wording and told Marshall to issue the order immediately. With a friendly laugh and an incredulous smile, Marshall asked, "Am I expected to believe that this is General Pershing's order, when I know damn well you came to this conclusion during our conversation?"

"That is the order of the Commander in Chief, which I am authorized to issue in his name," Connor replied. "Now get it out as quickly as possible."

Marshall demurred. The operation, after all, had been dictated by Ferdinand Foch, who was by mutual consent among the Allies the generalissimo of their collective endeavor. Marshall asked Connor for permission to delay the issuing order until six o'clock so that authorization from First Army commander Hunter Liggett and his chief of staff, Hugh A. Drum, could be obtained. If they could not be located in time to give authorization, Marshall told Connor that he would telephone the order to the pertinent commanders. Grudgingly, Connor agreed and departed.

Because every minute that passed favored the Germans, Marshall checked the whereabouts of Liggett and Drum every ten minutes. When Drum returned to the command post at five minutes before six, Marshall showed him the order. Drum approved it, but added that boundaries would "not be considered binding." This gave the U.S. First Corps tacit permission to cross the line separating it from the French Fourth Army.

The effect of the order on the U.S. First Corps and Fifth Corps was the same as if Marshall had fired a starter's pistol for a foot race.

"It did not authorize a free for all," Marshall said later, "although that is what happened."[4]

The scramble to take Sedan resulted in a case of mistaken identity and the capture by an American lieutenant of the AEF's most decorated general. As the stampede toward Sedan began with the First Division (the "Big Red One") moving forward on the night of November 5, 1918, soldiers who wore the shoulder patch with large red numeral one headed for territory held by Forty-second ("Rainbow") Division men wearing their rainbow patches. As the First Division and the Forty-second became hopelessly tangled, Brigadier General Douglas MacArthur, unaware of Pershing's (that is, Connor's) attack order, set out to investigate. Wearing a uniform of his own creation that violated army regulations in nearly every aspect, consisting of a crumpled hat in lieu of a helmet, long silk scarf, riding pants, and gleaming knee-high boots, he paused to study a map. Seeing him, a certain Lieutenant Black, leading a First Division patrol, concluded that anyone in a uniform he did not recognize as American or French must be German. He therefore drew his pistol and demanded surrender. Before long, First Brigade officer Hjalmar Erickson recognized the irate and protesting prisoner, apologized, and ordered MacArthur released.

In the end, neither the French nor the Americans would take Sedan. When the armistice took effect, at the eleventh hour of the eleventh day and the eleventh month—11 A.M., November 11—the city was still in German hands.

Colonel Marshall had even more lessons to learn. The last few days had taught him about the relation between battlefield realities and national honor and about the exigencies of command authority. He would now learn something about the direct connection between the muddy, bloody facts of trench warfare and global politics. He would get an inkling of the relationship between soldiering and diplomacy. In the world to which the world war had given birth, he would discover, it was no longer possible for a soldier to be purely a soldier. Like it or not, he was part of a larger global political reality.

While the generals made arrangements for the signing of armistice papers so that the diplomats of the victorious powers could hammer out peace terms to be dictated to the defeated, Marshall was an awestruck witness to a meal in AEF general headquarters at which the French attaché and the British army representative calmly discussed the distribution of Germany's colonies (in Africa and elsewhere) and the constituents of the Ottoman Empire. When the Frenchman proposed that the United States take Ottoman Syria, Marshall found himself chiming in that the United States was opposed to any colony that had a wet or dry season and an abnormal number of insects. Bermuda, he said, was the only colony the United States would possibly consider. It was, of course, a joke, the product of Marshall's disbelief that a pair of comparatively low-level military functionaries could divide the world among themselves. The Americans present at the table got the joke, and they were flabbergasted to note that the Englishman seemed to think that he had discovered, at last, just what America was after in the war.

That had been a joke. But at a breakfast with the same group on the morning of the armistice, the French attaché spoke of seeking revenge on Germany. And he was dead serious. As for the Englishman, he was still set on apportioning the colonies, as well as establishing "freedom of the seas," albeit under strict British supervision. Half an hour before all fighting was set to cease at 11:00 A.M., the mess hall was rocked by the explosion of a bomb that landed in the garden just outside the room's window. The blast blew everyone out of their chairs. Marshall landed on the floor, sitting on the back of his chair, with a bump on his head. His first thought was that he was dead, but, coming to his senses and surveying the room, he found that, aside from a ruined breakfast, no great damage had been done. A few minutes later, a young aviator burst in. He explained that he had been returning from a mission and a bomb that stuck in its rack had shaken loose right over the garden. He apologized.

Marshall later described this brush with death just thirty minutes before the armistice as a sort of parting thrill. In fact, it was perhaps the most important lesson about war. Strategy, tactics, honor, emotion, global politics—in the end, even a half hour before the end, war was really all about killing or being killed.

┼╾╼┼

Marshall's last days at First Army Headquarters required him to manage the deployment of troops to Germany for occupation duty. This involved shifting 600,000 men, but he noted that he had been working so long with such big issues and numbers in such rapid succession that no one even commented on the magnitude of the undertaking.

On November 19, Marshall returned to Chaumont as chief of staff of the new Eighth Army Corps, headquartered in the south of France in the village of Montigny.

In a chateau he chose as the residence of the corps commander, Major General Henry T. Allen, he arranged a Christmas Eve dinner, with Allen as the host to corps staff and several French neighbors, for whom this was the first celebration since 1914. Nervous and stiff at first, the French guests soon warmed to an American-style party and kept the festivities going until two in the morning.

Through eighteen months of war, George Catlett Marshall had not fired a shot. As the American Expeditionary Force in France swelled from thousands to hundreds of thousands, he learned how to disembark them, transport them inland, feed, billet, supply, and train them. He came to know the complexities and sensitivities of feelings—including national pride—in Allied warfare. He was as familiar as any general with the problems faced by a fighting force, and understood more about how to solve them than many men with stars on their collars. His battles were waged on paper and over the phone, but he had slogged through mud and been under fire at the front. He had seen the futility and waste of manhood in trench warfare, witnessed the military value of airplanes, and noted that another innovation, the tank, had made the horse cavalry an anachronism. He observed senior commanders who clung to the ways of the past and the young who looked to the future. As operations officer, he directed the movement of more combat troops than anyone in the history of American arms.

Pershing's chief of supply, General George Van Horn Moseley, would look back on the AEF's experience in the Great War and write of Marshall, "The troops which maneuvered under his plans always won."[5] Moseley was not alone in this insight. Not only would army high command recognize Marshall's value as a staff officer, a leader of staff officers, and a manager of armies, but, in significant measure *because* of Marshall, they would come to recognize that wars were not fought and won exclusively at the point of a bayonet. For the first time in its history, the United States military establishment would begin to afford the rear echelon the attention it deserved and modern warfare demanded. Under Marshall in the next world war, this doctrine would become paramount, and those who later failed to heed the lessons of creating a sustainable force and sustainable effort in warfighting would force the nation to pay a heavy price. That was the case in Iraq and Afghanistan under Secretary of Defense Donald H. Rumsfeld, whose Pentagon stretched the American military beyond its optimum effectiveness and very nearly beyond endurance.

CHAPTER 5

Little Black Book

AS THE PRACTICAL GENIUS OF GEORGE MARSHALL EMERGED, GENERAL John J. Pershing was there to make the fullest possible use of it. Like Marshall, Pershing understood and accepted the realities of warfare on the largest scale and did not allow himself to be intoxicated by the thrill of victory. Marshall had just settled at Montigny in the comforts of a twelfth-century chateau surrounded by beautiful grounds, graced by a little stream running beneath his window and the presence of a swan someone on General Allen's staff had christened "Mike," when he received Pershing's order to return to Chaumont. Peace talks were under way at Versailles. But what if they somehow and suddenly collapsed? The AEF commander wanted Marshall to work on a contingency plan to renew the war—just in case. The complicating factor was that the order came even as the AEF was rapidly shrinking under the American public's demand that "the boys" come home, and quickly.

Marshall proceeded to embrace the realities of demobilization just as he had those of war. In any case, the plan for resuming the war soon proved unnecessary. But Pershing's requirements of Marshall barely let up. As doughboys were being rapidly demobilized, the commanding general was hearing dismaying stories from friends in the United States that thousands of men who had been told that they were fighting to make the world "safe for democracy" (in the words of Woodrow Wilson's April 1917 address to Congress, asking for a declaration of war) were coming home with a woeful lack of understanding of what the war had been for.[1]

Pershing dispatched Marshall to French embarkation ports to personally deliver lectures designed to educate soldiers waiting to board U.S.-bound troopships.

It is a measure of Marshall's creative genius that he did not merely follow orders. Instead, he turned his assignment into an opportunity to inquire into soldiers' grievances and to get *their* assessment of the quality of their officers. When the troops of the Twenty-seventh Division complained about having to fill out the very same complicated paperwork and undergo the same inspections in the French port of Brest that they'd already completed at Le Mans, Marshall saw to it that such bureaucratic duplication ended. Most of the recommendations Marshall made for charges in army procedures, based on what he learned from the troops, Pershing accepted and put into effect. As for the lecture Marshall gave on the purpose and success of the AEF, complete with maps and charts, it was deemed so effective that Pershing arranged a performance for a contingent of visiting members of Congress, including Fiorello La Guardia, a congressman and an air corps major who piloted bombers on the Italian front and would go on to become New York's most celebrated mayor. Fifteen years after hearing Marshall speak, Major General John A. Lejeune, who commanded the Fourth Marine Brigade and then assumed command of the Army Second Division in the war, would write, "I learned more about the general history of the war than I have learned since."[2]

At a ceremony in the Place de la Republique in Metz on April 30, 1919, Marshall was awarded the Legion of Honor, France's accolade for distinguished service. Among other recipients was Colonel James L. Collins, Pershing's aide in the Philippines and Mexico, who had been with Black Jack early in the war but had returned to Washington. Assigned once again to Pershing's staff, he asked Marshall just before the medal ceremony, "How would you like to be the General's aide?" After the French award had been pinned to his uniform, Marshall told Collins that he would.

Following the signing of the peace accords at Versailles, Pershing's headquarters moved from Chaumont to Paris. Settled into the house of American banker Ogden Mills on the Rue de Varenne, Marshall, as Pershing's aide, found himself at the general's side as the governments of France and Britain expressed their relief at the war's end in a succession of celebrations, beginning with a Fourth of July review of American troops by French President Raymond Poincaré. In a victory parade on Bastille Day, Marshall rode a white horse from the Arc de Triomphe down the Champs Elysées to a reviewing stand in the Place de la Republique.

After spending the evening making the rounds of street dances, Pershing's staff left Paris at 1:00 A.M. by train, bound for Boulogne, where the British destroyer HMS *Orpheus* was waiting to ferry them across the English Channel to let the British people see the most famous victorious American general in whom they'd had a stake since George Washington. Following an evening of meeting and dining with dukes, duchesses, lords, ladies, a princess, and even the governor of Jerusalem, Marshall accompanied Pershing to the Whitehall offices of the British War Office to present the Distinguished Service Medal to civilian officials of the government, including the secretary of state for war, Winston Churchill. At a dinner for the Americans in the House of Commons, the forty-year-old colonel heard the Churchillian eloquence for the first time. The forty-five-year-old politician, author, journalist, and warrior—who had ridden in the last great cavalry charge during the Sudan campaign of 1898—declaimed, "From the moment the Germans in their vanity and folly drove the United States to draw the sword there was no doubt that Germany was ruined, that the cause of freedom was safe, and that the British and American democracy would begin once more to write their history in common."[3]

In a city where the staging of regal ceremonies had been going on for a thousand years, the colonel from Uniontown, General Pershing, and other officers in the army of an austere republic found themselves cheered, hailed, saluted, and embraced at luncheons and receptions in hotels, teas in aristocratic parlors, and at a Buckingham Palace garden party, where King George V and Queen Mary greeted them. Ever-appreciative of good-looking women, Marshall filled pages of a diary with descriptions and depictions of their lavish attire, especially the profusion of huge ostrich-feather fans all the women carried.

After a review of a regiment of American troops by the Prince of Wales, Marshall followed Pershing on an inspection of the arrayed ranks in Hyde Park, accompanied by Churchill. As they reached the end of a line of soldiers about to return to a country whose constitution had recently been amended to outlaw the sale, manufacture, and transportation of alcohol ("Prohibition"), Churchill exclaimed, "What a magnificent body of men never to take another drink."

Returning to France, Marshall, always at Pershing's side, attended yet more parades, parties, and salutes. The two men visited the First and Third divisions on occupation duty in Germany, made a nine-day tour of the battlefields of the Western Front, and then traveled to Italy for four days of tributes. After nine more days of farewells and packing in Paris, they arrived in Brest to board the SS *Leviathan,* which steamed for home on September 1, 1919.

As Marshall proceeded through a blizzard of tickertape in a parade down Broadway to New York's City Hall with Pershing and his staff and the marching ranks of First Division veterans of a world war that no one yet called the "first," he was disappointed that he had not been made a brigadier general. Although Pershing had sent a recommendation of promotion to Washington, the end of the war had brought a War Department decree that all those who held temporary ranks were reverted to their permanent grades. It would be eighteen years before he received his star.

Twenty-two years after enrolling at VMI to learn how to be an infantry officer, he had yet to lead men in combat. He had proved his excellence at planning operations, moving thousands of men into battle, and deftly handling logistics in response to situational changes. Superior competence had been rewarded with temporary promotions and added responsibilities to the point where he found himself aide-de-camp to the most honored general since Ulysses S. Grant. (On September 5, while at sea on the *Leviathan,* Pershing had received word that he had been promoted to general of the armies, an honor previously granted only to George Washington.) Greeting Pershing in 1919 were Vice President Thomas R. Marshall on behalf of President Wilson; Secretary of War Newton Baker; Army Chief of Staff General Peyton

March; General Bullard; New York Governor Alfred E. Smith; and New York City Mayor John F. Hylan. After New York, there were parades in Philadelphia and Washington, D.C., capped off by a joint session of Congress to honor the general. The triumph by the United States in the "war to end all wars" had been purchased for $23.5 billion and 116,708 American lives. Marshall would later say, "It always seemed that battles were inextricably connected with cold and rain, and mud and gloom."[4] Ten minutes of combat, he would state, was ten minutes too much. He had found war to be horribly and profoundly depressing.

Waiting to welcome him home among the crowd of officials at New York's City Hall was his wife, Lily. After two years, he found her as beautiful as ever, but she was still much too frail to risk a pregnancy. Reunion with the husband who was now aide-de-camp to Pershing meant leaving the cottage next to the VMI parade field in Lexington to live in Washington. Their first home together was an apartment in a residential hotel favored by military officers and a few bachelor congressmen at 2400 Sixteenth Street NW. In a city rapidly gearing down from wartime urgency for the peacetime "normalcy" promised by the 1920 Republican candidate for president, Warren G. Harding, dinner guests of the Marshalls found Lily to be a charming southern belle and her tall, handsome husband an amusing raconteur. Table talk across the city was of a stroke that had left President Wilson paralyzed, and there were rumors that his wife, Edith, was running the country. The capital also buzzed about a debate over how large an army the nation needed now that the world had a League of Nations to keep wars from breaking out. Of course, the League was without the presence of the United States because the Republican-controlled Senate had blocked ratification, thereby vetoing America's membership.

Pending before Congress was a proposal from Secretary of War Newton Baker and the army chief of staff, General Peyton March, for a standing army of 500,000. At Pershing's request, Marshall collaborated with Fox Connor to craft a proposal for a smaller regular army force to be backed up by the National Guard and reserves. To ensure a supply of qualified reservists, Marshall and Connor added a proposal to give all young men eleven months of universal military training (UMT), after which they would be obligated to reserve service for four years. In testimony before the joint House and Senate committee on military affairs on October 31 and November 1, 1919, Pershing presented the plan, which specified a regular army of 300,000 men augmented by the Guard and trained reserves.

Both Marshall and Connor attended the Capitol Hill testimony. It was Marshall's first close-up view of the civilian oversight of the military in a democracy, and it was sobering. The Great War had been followed by a veritable tidal wave of isolationism and pacifism that swept the country and certainly doomed the UMT proposal. Marshall nevertheless remained a strong believer in the principle, and some three decades after Congress rejected UMT in 1919, he would again advocate strenuously for it, persuading President Harry Truman in March 1948 to formally propose it. (Although the Military Training and Service Act of 1951 would be less than Marshall had wanted, it would embody much of what he had championed. The draft eligibility age was lowered from nineteen to eighteen and a half, the period of service was increased from twenty-one to twenty-four months, and the total service obligation, active plus reserve, was fixed at eight years. The 1951 legislation also approved UMT, at least in principle, authorizing passage of additional legislation to induct youths for six months of service in a "National Security Training Corps." Marshall expressed confidence that Congress would eventually enact the necessary UMT legislation, but, in fact, it never did.)

Pershing drew heavily on Marshall's research and compilation work to prepare his official after-action report on the American Expeditionary Force, which was released in December 1919. With this completed, Pershing looked forward to release from the army. He was seriously contemplating a bid for the White House, something of which Marshall disapproved; he believed that career military men had no place in partisan civilian politics. He thought that, on the one hand, Pershing the war hero would end up like Grant the war hero, sullied by inevitable political corruption; on the other hand, Marshall also feared that the qualities that made for a great military commander threatened democracy when transferred to the civilian sphere. When Secretary of War Newton Baker forced Pershing to delay his retirement by asking that he tour army camps and industrial plants and make recommendations as to which ones should be retained, Pershing put all of the planning in the hands of Marshall, Connor, and General George Van Horn Moseley, then resumed his own plans for a presidential candidacy. But when a delegation of Tennessee Republicans came to talk to Pershing about running, Marshall sent them away, explaining that the general was out.

When Pershing learned about this, he was furious, but after Ohio Senator Warren G. Harding attained the Republican nomination, Pershing brushed aside suggestions that he run as a Democrat and simply gave up the idea of running at all, declaring that under no circumstances would he consider being a candidate.

Thus Pershing remained in the army and, after Harding's election, succeeded Peyton March as army chief of staff. Marshall, who had reverted to his prewar rank of captain and then received promotion to major, was installed as the chief's aide in an office in the former State, War, and Navy departments Building immediately west of the White House. Pershing enjoyed his authority as the army's senior officer, but he had little interest in most peacetime administrative routine and therefore assigned Marshall a level of responsibility not customarily entrusted to an aide. To a significant degree, Pershing became a figurehead, and it was Marshall who effectively functioned as the true head of the army. It was a challenge, to be sure, but in great measure a thankless one, since he had to contend with a postwar mixture of apathy and animosity from the public and Congress alike concerning the military's needs. Still, proximity to power had its perks. As chief of staff, Pershing resided in Quarters No. 1 at the U.S. Army's plum posting, the elegant Fort Myer in Virginia, across the Potomac River from the capital and adjacent to Arlington National Cemetery. Marshall and Lily lived in Quarters No. 3 and slipped easily into the post's vibrant social life and dinner parties and receptions in the capital. Marshall rubbed elbows with the most powerful figures in the nation's military and the civilian government. Officially Fort Myer was designated a cavalry post, and, by way of recreation, Marshall enjoyed almost daily rides through the facility's many pleasant bridle paths.

When he wasn't running the army or riding through Fort Myer, Marshall wrote his own memoir of the war. He submitted it to the Houghton Mifflin publishing house, but when an editor there asked for revisions, Marshall took it to mean that the manuscript was unworthy and put it aside. It would lie untouched in an old footlocker until Marshall's stepdaughter, Molly Brown Winn, ran across it many years later in the attic of Marshall's home in Leesburg, Virginia. She had long believed that it had been destroyed at Marshall's request. The book was published by Houghton Mifflin in 1976 as *Memoirs of My Services in the World War, 1917–1918,* with a foreword and notes by Brigadier General James Lawton Collins Jr., chief of military history for the Department of the Army (and the son of James Lawton Collins, who in 1919 had asked Marshall if he wanted to be General Pershing's aide.)

Marshall, who had reverted to his prewar Regular Army rank of captain in September 1919 and was promoted to Regular Army major in July 1920, became an RA lieutenant colonel in August 1923 and accompanied Pershing on a national tour of army camps. While in San Francisco, the two men received word that President Harding had died in San Francisco while returning from a visit to Alaska, and that they were assigned to accompany the funeral train back to Washington. As aide to Pershing, Marshall had walked the short distance from the War Department to the White House for long conversations with Harding on military policy and talks pertaining to the size of the army in a democracy in peacetime. These meetings were typical of many Marshall attended alongside Pershing. Among the powerful men he met in company with Pershing was the financier Bernard Baruch, perennial presidential adviser, a man whose input would be influential through the Roaring Twenties, the Great Depression, World War II, and the Cold War (a label he popularized in a 1947 speech to the South Carolina legislature). He would become both Marshall's close friend and influential adviser.

During the Harding years, Marshall had also dealt extensively with Assistant Secretary of the Navy Theodore (Ted) Roosevelt, Jr. Having returned from the war to help form the American Legion, Ted Roosevelt had become the number two man in the Navy Department, following in the footsteps of his father, who had held the post under President William McKinley, as well as those of his distant cousin, Franklin Delano Roosevelt, who had the same post under Woodrow Wilson. In a meeting with Ted Roosevelt to advocate steps to help the two branches understand each other's problems, Marshall proposed an exchange of officers in which they would perform each other's jobs in supply, ordnance, and communication. This innovative idea, which anticipated by decades the unification of the military under a single Department of Defense, met with fervent opposition from both Navy and Army departments.

In 1924, with Pershing on the verge of retirement, George Marshall, having attained the Regular Army rank of lieutenant colonel, seized on the long-elusive opportunity to lead troops. The assignment was with the elite Fifteenth Infantry in Tientsin, China, part of the force the Western powers had imposed on China after the Boxer Rebellion of 1900. It was without question the most desirable overseas posting in the peacetime army.

On July 12, Marshall, with Lily and her mother, sailed from New York aboard the U.S. Army Transport (USAT) fittingly named *St. Mihiel.* Sailing via the Panama Canal, the *St. Mihiel* docked in San Francisco, where Marshall and his party transferred to the USAT *Thomas,* which arrived in China on September 7. Tientsin was sixty miles up the Hai River from the seacoast and was laid out astride the strategically critical Peking-Mukden Railroad. The U.S. government paid rent for the Tientsin cantonment of the Fifteenth Regiment (on a site vacated by the Germans in 1919), and its 850 officers and men were assigned to keep the railroad open and operating during chronic episodes of warfare between Chinese warlords and their factions contending for control of the virtually nonexistent central government.

On his arrival, Marshall learned that the regiment's commander had been posted back to the States, and because his replacement had yet to arrive, he would be in command of troops himself for the first time. It was only garrison duty, and it was only until the replacement arrived, but it *was* command of two battalions of the Fifteenth "Can Do" Regiment at an overseas post, and Marshall reveled in it. In addition to wearing the required ceremonial sword, he started carrying a swagger stick, a habit many officers had picked up from the British during the Great War. Among the officers of the Fifteenth were Captain Matthew B. Ridgway and Major Joseph W. Stilwell, both destined for greatness in World War II.

Marshall had hardly finished unpacking when he was informed that elements of a defeated Chinese factional army were descending on Tientsin from the north. Flooding south on hijacked trains, commandeered river streamers, mules, horses, and on foot were thousands of heavily armed, hungry, leaderless men. Ordering a corporal and five soldiers to each of five posts on the city's outskirts, with a team of Chinese to help them, Marshall instructed them to offer the fleeing troops rice, boiled cabbage, and tea in exchange for surrender of their weapons. Ridgway recalled that Marshall's instruction to him was to use bluff, expostulation, or entreaty, but under no circumstances was he to fire unless fired upon. The tactic worked. There was no shooting. The Chinese troops bypassed the city and continued their movement southward, some dispersing, others doubtless joining other factions under other warlords.

Such alarms were rare. Settled with Lily and her mother in a ten-room house with a large staff of servants in the U.S. compound on Woodrow Wilson Street, Marshall passed mostly pleasant days riding on a shaggy Mongolian pony, playing squash and tennis, and learning passable Chinese. Lily also enjoyed the comfortable lifestyle and relished collecting Chinese furnishings and art, but her fragile physical condition always limited her exertions. Despite the country's tumultuous political and military situation, she saw more of her husband than she had since before the Great War.

If Marshall achieved little that was memorable during his three-year China tour, such was the nature of garrison duty. As the end of the assignment approached, he longed to become assistant commandant of the Infantry School at Fort Benning, Georgia, but the order that came instead was duty as a lecturer at the Army War College in Washington. The family departed for home in May 1927 and settled back in Washington in August. Almost immediately, Lily's heart condition took a turn for the worse, and she entered Walter Reed General Hospital for tests. Discovering that she suffered from a goiter (an enlargement of the thyroid gland), surgeons operated on August 21. Her recovery proved difficult and lengthy, but when a doctor told her on September 15 that she could go home the next day, Lily was thrilled. She sat at the desk in her hospital room to write the good news in a note to her mother. Her heart stopped before she could finish it. The last word she wrote was "George."

A War College guard interrupted Marshall's lecture to tell him that he was wanted urgently on the telephone. While the guard stood by, Marshall sat at a desk, spoke on the phone for a moment, then lowered his head and rested it in his arms. The worried guard asked if he could do anything for him. "No," Marshall replied. "I just had word my wife has just died."

Replying to a condolence letter from Pershing, who had lost his wife and three of his four children in a house fire at the Presidio in 1915, Marshall wrote, "The truth is, the thought of all you had endured gave me heart and hope. But twenty-six years of most intimate companionship, something I have known since I was a mere boy, leaves me lost in my best effort to adjust to future prospects in life. If I had been given to club life or other intimacies with men outside of athletic diversions, or if there was a campaign or other pressing duty demanding a concentrated effort, then I think I should do better. However, I will find a way."[5]

In this period of anguish, he confided to a friend that he thought he might explode if he did not find a job to occupy him mentally and physically. Army Chief of Staff Charles P. Summerall gave his World War operations officer the option of staying on at the War College, transferring to New York's Governors Island as a corps operations officer, or filling a vacancy at the Infantry School, Fort Benning, Georgia. Summerall explained that as the result of Colonel Frank S. Cocheu's ending his tour as assistant commandant, Marshall would have virtually complete charge of Fort Benning's Academic Department. He would control the curriculum for teaching small-unit tactics to company-grade officers. He would also be able to experiment with new infantry techniques and battlefield mobility. It was the very job he wanted, and, coming at such a terrible time, he felt that it had saved his life.

Nine miles from the sleepy town of Columbus, Georgia, Fort Benning sprawled over 97,000 acres along the Chattahoochee River. Marshall arrived in early November 1927 and threw himself into the new job, which offered a limitless field of activity and a professional faculty eager to learn and to teach new ways of doing things. When he wasn't in his office or a classroom, Marshall made a garden in the yard of the house, went riding by the river, and, over time, organized the Fort Benning Hunt with a pack of hounds and nearly a hundred officers and their wives on horses thundering across the Georgia meadows and woods.

In classrooms, his goal was a thorough revision of the means of instruction, in which the greatest of his lessons was the need for simplicity in the techniques professional officers used to lead troops of a citizen army. He stressed that in the field it was the unexpected that was normal and that officers had to be ready for anything. Unlike so many officers who had led combat units in the fixed trenches of the Western Front and who therefore had an idea of warfare as static, Marshall taught a war of movement dominated by the tank and airplane. Yes, the trench dominated the World War, but the emergence of the tank, the plane, and other vehicles during that conflict meant that the next war would not be fought in trenches but on the move. Accordingly, Marshall ordered a special tank battalion to be attached to Fort Benning, and he arranged for demonstrations of air support by a squadron from nearby Maxwell Field. Along with movement and speed came a need for nimble improvisation, a skill he sought to imbue in students and instructors alike. No instructor was permitted to read prepared lectures. They were to teach spontaneously. To teach improvisation, they were to teach *by* improvisation.

Among those who came to teach under Marshall was Captain J. (Joseph) Lawton Collins (not to be confused with Pershing's former aide James Lawton Collins, mentioned above), who had arrived fresh from Field Artillery School at Fort Sill, Oklahoma, in August 1927. Told to expect in Marshall a grave and humorless man, Collins was raking leaves in front of his Benning cottage one Saturday afternoon when Marshall walked by. "He stopped to chat," Collins later wrote, "and as he seemed to linger, I invited him in for a cup of tea. I said Mrs. Collins probably was not dressed for visitors, but he accepted without hesitation. Gladys served us tea, and the Colonel sat and visited for some while in a relaxed, informal fashion. Thereafter I always felt at ease with this remarkable man."

Collins became one of Marshall's many admirers at Fort Benning. He acknowledged that his predecessors had launched the new Infantry School in 1918, but that Marshall's arrival marked its coming of age. He explained that Marshall brought a fresh outlook on problems of the infantry, and, indeed, brought a fresh outlook to the entire army. He marveled at the maturity of Marshall's innovative judgments and his certainty as to what he wanted to accomplish, including ridding the infantry of its knee-jerk conservative ways and instead developing new ideas and methods. Collins recalled that Marshall made it clear to the faculty and students that everything was subject to challenge. He told the faculty that any student's solution to a problem that differed markedly from the approved solution, yet made sense, should be published to the class.

"Despite Colonel Marshall's seemingly forbidding appearance," wrote Collins, "he was always accessible. Anyone with a new idea, a new method or procedure, could get a hearing and was encouraged to come up with a specific project to develop his theory. [He] frequently sat in on faculty lectures and listened in on the discussions, getting a feel for students and instructors. As he came to know the faculty, he gradually made changes."[6] These changes included bringing Joseph W. Stilwell to Benning from China in 1930 to head the tactical section, which included Collins. Marshall's choice to head the weapons section was Major Omar N. Bradley. A West Point graduate (1915), Bradley had troop experience in the West (1915–1919), which was followed by extensive teaching experience, with the ROTC in Minnesota and South Dakota (1919–1920) and as an instructor in mathematics at West Point (1920–1924). Like Marshall, he had not served in a combat leadership role and therefore, also like Marshall, he was not wedded to the static ideas of trench warfare. Bradley would become one of Marshall's acolytes, an advocate of everything associated with the warfare of movement and maneuver.

Marshall came to believe that the Infantry School faculty he assembled during his last three years as the assistant commandant was the most brilliant, interesting, and thoroughly competent collection of men with whom he had ever been associated. They thought seriously about the future of the U.S. Army and the future of warfighting. They were not afraid to look outside the accepted field for help in solving problems of national defense. They became known as "Marshall's Men," the central figures in what came to be called the "Benning Revolution." It would lay the foundation of warfighting doctrine for World War II, and it turned out the generation of company-grade officers who would fight that war. The lieutenants and captains who left the Infantry School left bearing Marshall's imprint. They were imbued with the pragmatism of applying tested principles and common sense to battlefield situations, and with an understanding that one day, they would almost certainly be called upon to lead not professional soldiers, but an army of citizen soldiers. As for their instructors, Marshall entered their names into what he called "my little black book." These were the men he wanted as future brigade, battalion, division, corps, and army commanders. Among them were most of the great names of the American army of World War II: Bradley, Collins, Ridgway, Stilwell, James Van Fleet, Terry Allen, Norman Cota, Clarence Huebner, and Walter Bedell Smith. In all, fifty instructors and 150 students of Marshall's Infantry School became generals in the next world war. And it was also thanks to Marshall—and his leading apostle Bradley—that professional education and training became a central focus of the U.S. Army. Today, no institution in the world, public or private, educates more men and women than America's army.

Less than a year after becoming the assistant commandant of the Infantry School and while still recovering from the death of Lily, Marshall learned from his sister Marie that their mother had died of a heart attack at Marie's home in Greensburg, Pennsylvania. Within the next year, Lily's mother also died. The loss within two years of the three most important women in his life left George Marshall feeling lonelier than at any other time in his forty-nine years. He found relief through work and such diversions as riding with other officers and staging "pageants" for visiting dignitaries in place of traditional (and tedious) military reviews. The pageants consisted of a series of "acts" presenting the various activities of the post in which students paraded with their weapons, tennis players with their rackets, polo players with their horses, and basketball and baseball teams with their equipment. Because his house was next to the tennis courts, he often invited players in for refreshments. To the children of officers' families this customarily reserved figure became known as "Uncle George."

Lonely though he might be, Marshall had many friends who frequently invited him to their homes. Asked to a dinner party by a civilian acquaintance in Columbus in the autumn of 1929, he was told that the only other guests would be the hostess's widowed former college friend and her teenage daughter. When they arrived, Marshall was standing by the fireplace. As the widow crossed the room, she saw him decline an offered drink. Smiling as she approached, she said, "You are a rather unusual Army officer, aren't you? I have never known one to refuse a cocktail before."

Marshall asked how many army officers she knew.

She replied, "Not many."

Recently, the men Katherine Boyce Tupper Brown had known were lawyers. Born in Harrodsburg, Kentucky, in October 1882, she graduated from Hollins College, near Roanoke, Virginia, in 1904, then shocked her father, uncles, and grandfather, all Baptist ministers, by studying at the American Academy of Dramatic Arts in New York City and at the Comédie Française in Paris. As Katherine Boyce, she became a noted Shakespearean actress in Ireland and in London. Just when her stage career was blossoming, she began suffering from severe bouts of pain. After being stricken twice while on stage, she was diagnosed as suffering from tuberculosis of the kidney. On her return to the United States, however, physicians told her that her only problem was physical exhaustion, and she was sent to rest in the Adirondack Mountains. There she was visited by a childhood friend from Baltimore, Clifton S. Brown, who, declaring his lifelong love, proposed marriage. Having just received an offer to join the company of the eminent actor Richard Mansfield, she turned Brown down and went to Chicago. But after several performances, the pains returned, and one night she was stricken so severely after the final curtain that she was unable to move and had to be carried from the stage. She returned to the Adirondacks rest cure and, once again, was courted by Clifton Brown. Pressured by worried family and friends to quit acting, this time she accepted his proposal.

In the decade of a booming stock market in which President Calvin Coolidge proclaimed that "the chief business of the American people is business," Katherine Boyce Tupper Brown was the vivacious wife of a successful Baltimore lawyer and champion tennis player and the mother of three children, Molly, Clifton Jr., and Allen. With arresting looks, a professionally acquired English accent, and an actress's poise, she was a gracious hostess at dinners and cocktail parties in the family's Baltimore home. For summers and weekend getaways, she had enough money of her own to buy a getaway cottage on New York's Fire Island (off of Long Island). It seemed the culmination of the good life, and the day the deed to the property arrived, Katherine phoned her husband's office to tell him the exciting news. No one answered. A short time later, a pair of Baltimore police detectives knocked on her door. They regretted to inform her that her husband had been accosted by a disgruntled client in the foyer of his office. The man drew a pistol. The point-blank shot was fatal.

For the next year, Katherine dealt with her shock and grief by staying with a sister in the quiet seclusion of Connecticut and with Molly in a cottage on Waikiki Beach in Hawaii. On their way back to Baltimore, she decided to pay a visit to Molly's godmother, Mrs. William Randolph Blanchard, in Columbus, Georgia. That is when her former college classmate invited her and Molly to dinner. Reluctant at first, she changed her mind when the friend said there would be only her husband, herself, and, "Lieutenant Colonel George C. Marshall, from Fort Benning."

Her first impression of him was of a tall, slender man with sandy hair and deep-set eyes. As they dined, she decided, "This certainly was someone different."

Marshall felt the same about her and asked to drive her home. After an hour in which he seemed to have gotten lost, she asked, "How long have you been at Fort Benning?"

He replied, "Two years."

"Well," she said, "after two years haven't you learned your way around Columbus?"

"Extremely well," he said confidently, "or I could not have stayed off the block where Mrs. Blanchard lives."

Although both had more than once declared their determination not to marry again, they began an exchange of letters. During the summer of 1929, while on temporary duty in Wyoming, Marshall wrote to Mrs. Blanchard to suggest that she invite Katherine to Columbus again. When the reunion occurred in the spring of 1930, Marshall proposed, and Katherine accepted— pending, she said, the approval of her children, which she readily received from Molly and Clifton Jr. After she told twelve-year-old Allen that she was thinking of inviting Marshall to join them at Fire Island, the boy said they should leave things as they were. But the following morning, he told her it was all right and wrote to Marshall: "I hope you will come to Fire Island. Don't be nervous. It's O.K. with me. A friend in need is a friend indeed, Allen Brown."

After five weeks on Fire Island, Marshall wrote to General Pershing about a mid-October marriage in which Marshall would acquire a complete family. With the aging hero of the Great War as best man, and Marshall's sister, Lily's brother Edmund Coles, and Katherine's sister Allene in the wedding party, the ceremony was held on October 15, 1930, in the chapel of Emmanuel Episcopal Church in Baltimore.

By the time Marshall neared the end of his tour at Fort Benning in 1931, Katherine decided she had become a pretty good army wife. Marshall had been offered the post of chief of constabulary in the Philippines and the superintendency of VMI, but he declined both, agreeing with Pershing's counsel that he should stay in the army. Still yearning to command troops, he welcomed orders assigning him to take charge of a battalion of the Eighth Infantry at the small post of Fort Screven, Georgia, beginning in July 1932.

At this time the U.S. Army was once again among the smallest in the world. Postwar demobilization and reductions resulting from congressional funding cuts forced depleted divisions to train as mere battalions or companies. Dispersion of the skeletonized divisions, brigades, and regiments among a large number of posts, many of them relics of the bygone Indian Wars, became a serious hindrance to the training of Regular Army personnel, although they were helpful in the training of the citizen soldiers of the National Guard. Because efforts to abandon small posts met with stubborn opposition from local interests and their representatives in Congress, the twenty-four regiments available for field service in the infantry of 1930 were spread thinly among forty-five posts, with one battalion or less at thirty-four of them. Most of the organic transportation of these units was of World War vintage, and the army did not have the money to concentrate them for training by other means. Although Marshall was to be in command of only 400 men, he wrote to Pershing, "However small, it at least keeps me away from office work and high theory."[7]

CHAPTER 6

America the Unready

"IT WAS A VERY SMALL COMMAND," KATHERINE MARSHALL remembered, "but George was glad to be back with troops after four years of Army schools."[1]

On the northern tip of Tybee Island and separated from the city of Savannah, Georgia, by a seventeen-mile drive through marshlands, edged on either side by windblown palm trees and hibiscus, Fort Screven struck Katherine as rather dilapidated after Benning. Recognizing that the small post needed sprucing up, Marshall noted on morning horseback rides which places could be improved by some flowers or a coat of paint. One of the men compared his attention to the condition of the post to that of a southern planter looking after his estate.

Because Congress had ignored President Hoover's request that army and navy personnel be exempted from a ten-percent pay cut imposed on all government employees, Marshall helped the Fort Screven soldiers make ends meet by directing the cooks in post kitchens to prepare extra portions of midday meals so the men could buy the food at cost to take home for family suppers.

To overcome any prideful resistance among the men to taking charity, Katherine noted, the Marshalls partook of the meal themselves until the custom was well established, even though she was financially able to enroll her sons in private schools and send Molly on a long trip around the world.

While Lieutenant Colonel Marshall worked to alleviate the difficult conditions under which his men served in the third year of the nation's worst economic depression, the American people were engaged in the quadrennial exercise of electing a president. Their choice in November was between a second term for President Herbert Hoover or a first term for the Democratic governor of New York, Franklin D. Roosevelt. How Marshall felt about the choice is not known. Like many professional military officers, he scrupulously kept his political views to himself. Nevertheless, although he was in Washington, D.C. on strictly private business on March 3, 1933, Marshall made it a point to take his place among the large crowd that gray morning to watch the Pennsylvania Avenue parade saluting FDR's inauguration. With the branches of the services leading off, Chief of Staff General Douglas MacArthur was followed by the display of flags of the First Division, inspiring in Marshall memories of France. Then came ranks of Knickerbocker Greys, young New Yorkers in cadet uniforms; U.S. Marines in clean white caps; sailors in blue jackets; soldiers in khaki, with khaki trucks, khaki antiaircraft guns, and a new kind of short black machine gun. There were blue Richmond Blues, gray Richmond Grays, and the red and gray Richmond Howitzers, all with white plumes and pre–Civil War uniforms. A passing band playing "The West Point Cadets' March" and "The Stars and Stripes Forever" brought back the America of Marshall's boyhood and young manhood. Then came the airplanes against the dark sky, flying in combat formations of nine, just as they had under General Billy Mitchell, massed in their hundreds over the Meuse-Argonne, presaging a new kind of warfare.

Within days of Marshall's return to Fort Screven, the new president signed a bill creating the Civilian Conservation Corps (CCC) to give thousands of young men government jobs planting trees and working on antiflood and erosion projects under army supervision. On May 10, 1933, the War Department was ordered to plan for the movement of 250,000 trainees into work camps by July 1. Named commanding officer of the Eighth Infantry, Marshall was promoted to Regular Army full colonel and named commanding officer of CCC District F of the IV Corps area (Georgia and

Florida), headquartered at Fort Moultrie on Sullivan's Island, three miles from Charleston.

The huge house assigned to the Marshalls had been built by the Coast Artillery. Finding it in bad repair, Katherine and a seamstress made up 325 yards of curtaining for its forty-two French doors. To decorate its many large rooms, Mrs. Marshall had a truckload of her antiques brought down from Baltimore in the belief that they were settled for at least two years. But the week that the last curtains were being hung, Marshall received orders to report for duty with the Illinois National Guard's Thirty-third Division headquartered in Chicago. Marshall wrote to MacArthur with a plea to be left in command of troops. It was the only time in his army career that he asked for special consideration, but the chief of staff replied with an explanation of why he believed a man of Marshall's talents had a duty to go where he was needed. The Illinois National Guard might be required to suppress civil disorder, MacArthur explained, to quell possible riots by unemployed men in a city severely hit by the Great Depression. Training for immediate readiness was required, and Marshall was the man to do it.

Unhappy to be given a training assignment, and dispirited about having to give up country living for city life, Marshall settled into an apartment with Katherine on the city's Near North Side near the Drake Hotel from which he took a thirty-minute daily walk to National Guard headquarters in the Loop, with an occasional horseback ride in the armory or tennis or squash matches for exercise at the Chicago Athletic Club. In fact, Marshall had ample leisure time to supervise the editing of the division's publication, *Illinois Guardsman.* This at least gave him pleasure and satisfaction. Katherine remarked that he was as enthusiastic and energetic an editor as if he were responsible for *Time* magazine.

After a year in the city, the Marshalls found a house thirty-eight miles west, near Wayne, Illinois. Named White Gate Farm Cottage, close to Durham Woods Country Club, it allowed Marshall to ride and to breathe good country air on weekends. Commuting into the city by train, he had time to read newspaper accounts of the continuing Japanese aggression in Manchuria, Mussolini's invasion of Ethiopia in October 1935, Hitler's reconstituted military marching into the Rhineland, and Germany, Italy, and Russia all testing their militaries in the ongoing Spanish Civil War. Marshall's assignment was to train troops for domestic riot duty, but he couldn't help but realize that the U.S. Army was even more unprepared for war than it had been in 1917, and the world news certainly made another war seem likely.

⊱────⊰

Marshall did get an opportunity to lead troops during 1936 maneuvers in Michigan, when he served as commander of the "enemy" force. The exercise lasted two weeks, and involved 24,000 men and 2,000 officers of the Illinois and the Michigan National Guard as well as some Regular Army personnel. Writing to a friend that he had never learned more in his life in a similar period of time, Marshall said that war games had taught him the impracticality of most current U.S. Army tactics and theories—the very doctrine he had sought to purge through his stewardship of the Infantry School at Fort Benning. Officers whose experience of war was founded in the trenches could not seem to get that static model out of their minds. They based maneuvers on the assumption that the next war would necessarily resemble the Great War: and that it would consist of opposing armies dug into position, alternately attacking, defending, and counterattacking. In the Great War, the technology of defense, especially the trench and the machine gun, were more fully developed than the technology of attack. But by the end of that war, the latter had developed apace. The tank and other armored vehicles and the airplane were shifting the advantage from the defenders to the attackers. Yet in the Michigan maneuvers, no one in charge seemed to realize this. They planned and fought as if mobile warfare was an impossibility, as though the tank and the airplane did not exist, or, at least, as if they would play no meaningful role in any future conflict.

In an army of anachronisms and outmoded, even discredited, methods, not to mention stifling seniority regulations, Marshall felt strongly that he had been and was being held back by training assignments while men who had been his students had commanded troops and surpassed him in grade. He had been nominated for brigadier general in 1918 by General Pershing himself, only to have the promotion canceled when the war ended and officers with temporary grades reverted to their prewar rank. To regain the silver eagle of full colonel had taken eighteen years, despite his history of glowing efficiency reports and his legendary reputation for brilliant staff work and teaching. "I have possessed myself in patience," he wrote to Pershing two days after Christmas 1935, "but I'm fast getting too old to have any future of importance in the Army. This sounds pessimistic, but an approaching birthday—December 31—rather emphasizes the growing weakness of my position."[2]

His desire was to gain the two stars of major general before reaching the mandatory age of retirement (sixty-four) in 1944, yet in the autumn of 1935 he had yet to win the single star of a brigadier general. Indeed, even now, his ambition extended to becoming a four-star general as army chief of staff. Pershing and MacArthur were examples of men who had leap-frogged to the rank of full general (indeed, as noted above, Pershing held the almost unprecedented rank of "general of the armies"), but they had benefited from wartime promotions that, unlike his, were made permanent. Marshall knew that the only exceptions to the seniority rule were to be had through direct intervention by a general or a politician. While the record shows that Pershing was sympathetic to Marshall's sense of urgency in the matter of obtaining his first star and had even made appeals to Secretary of War George Dern and President Roosevelt, it proved to be a hard slog. General MacArthur was certainly reluctant to set aside a seniority system that had served the army for so long. Whether he was also averse to advancing to a higher spot on the promotion list anyone from the "Chaumont" crowd—Pershing's AEF inner circle, from which MacArthur had been excluded—cannot be verified. MacArthur did go on record to declare his intention to name Marshall chief of infantry, with the *temporary* rank of major general, at some point in the future, but he never got more specific than that.

At last, in April 1936, Pershing informed Marshall that Secretary Dern had agreed to put him on the September list for promotion to brigadier general, but that his (Pershing's) efforts to get him placed in a more advantageous position to get a second star ahead of others proved impossible. Indeed, by the time it came, the promotion to brigadier general was made only a month earlier than Marshall would have gotten it in the normal progress of the seniority system.

With the promotion came a change of post. He was to be commander of the Fifth Brigade, Third Division, at the Vancouver Barracks in the state of Washington. The assignment included supervising CCC camps in Washington and Oregon. In a brand-new Packard, and with an Irish terrier named "Pontiac," Marshall set out from Illinois in early October with Katherine and Molly on a three-week westward sightseeing odyssey of historical spots.

Happily in command of troops and reunited with a man he had known in the Philippines thirty-four years earlier (Henry Hossfield, now a colonel), Brigadier General Marshall made an effort to get to know the locals, as he had at Forts Screven and Moultrie. He traveled all over the Northwest with a cooking outfit in the back of the car and Katherine at his side to visit far-flung CCC camps. "We would be down in the valleys, a riot of color with wild flowers blooming everywhere, like a carpet covering the earth with glory," Katherine wrote, "and the next hour we would be high up in snow-covered mountains with great canyons at our sides; then down again through the lava, where Nature had twisted the earth into the likeness of the inferno."

Two events disrupted this idyll.

The first was a recurrence of a thyroid problem he had suffered at Fort Benning and that had flared up again in Chicago. After undergoing tests at Vancouver, Marshall was sent to San Francisco for surgery to remove his thyroid gland. Although he hoped to keep this secret from the army, gossip quickly spread through the highest echelons that he was seriously ill. To counter these possibly career-ending tales, he stepped up his vigorous daily exercise routines and made it widely known that a board of medical examiners had certified him fit for full duty.

The second event was an unexpected visit by a trio of Russian aviators who swooped out of the sky from the north. During a highly publicized flight from Moscow over the North Pole to Oakland, California, they ran out of fuel and landed at Pearson Field south of the Vancouver Barracks parade ground. As Marshall hastily left to meet them, he asked Katherine to make them breakfast and provide beds. "Twenty minutes later," she recalled, "three polar bears walked, or more exactly, staggered into our home. They wore huge parkas of fur, only their faces showing and these were so streaked with oil and dirt, so haggard and covered with beards, that the men hardly looked human."[3]

Within hours, all Vancouver Barracks turned into what Katherine called "a circus" as the Soviet ambassador to the United States, Washington and Oregon officials, the mayor of Portland and his staff, and dozens of reporters, photographers, and newsreel cameramen arrived to greet the aerial celebrities. Marshall set up an impromptu newsroom in his study, brought in telephones, and turned the living room over to radio networks for interviews with the Russians.

In the meantime, Marshall was hearing that, half a world away, in Moscow, Joseph Stalin was carrying out a purge of the Red Army's highest echelons, while in Berlin, Adolf Hitler was courting his military chiefs and making the German army the biggest in Europe. Directly from a former instructor at Fort Benning, Major Truman Smith, now serving as U.S. military attaché in Berlin, came a report that Hermann Göring, the German flying ace of the Great War who was now head of the Luftwaffe, had been assured that German aircraft factories were capable of producing 6,000 planes a year. In the United States in 1936, Major General Oscar Westover's Army Air Corps consisted of slightly less than 17,000 planes, many of them obsolescent, with 476 to be added within the next two years. At this rate, the strength of the Luftwaffe would soon eclipse that of the United States, and, what is more, the German planes would be of the very latest design.

Unlike his predecessors Harding, Coolidge, and Hoover, Franklin Roosevelt was no isolationist. At the urging of this former assistant secretary of the navy, Congress was beginning to fund the expansion of the American military, and the Roosevelt administration had recently issued the "Protective Mobilization Plan of 1937." The first step in expanding the army to meet what the White House perceived as a growing threat to national security was to be the federalization of the National Guard to provide with the Regular Army an "Initial Protective Force" of about 400,000. Together with the navy, this defensive force was to protect the nation while the army engaged in an orderly, staged expansion to wartime strength of one, two, and four million, as judged necessary. In principle, the plan was not all that different from today's integrated force concept, which has erased many of the distinctions among Regular Army, National Guard, and Army Reserve forces. The key difference between 1937 and today is the relative degree of readiness among the National Guard and reserve components. In 1937, this readiness was far more an aspiration than a reality. Today, it is a fact, as the army relies heavily on reserve components, especially the National Guard, for active combat duty. In 1935, Congress passed the first in a series of Neutrality Acts. Isolationists regarded them as a means of staying out of the war that was brewing in Europe, but by 1937, the military relied on them not to keep out of war, but to hold war off and buy time to build up the Regular Army component while also bringing the reserve components to a higher state of readiness. Unfortunately, the Neutrality Acts also had the effect of diminishing in many quarters what should have been a sense of urgency during a rapidly deteriorating global situation.

For the most part, during the late 1930s, the eyes of America's political and military planners were fixed on Germany and Italy. Marshall, however, who had a keen interest in China, noted that in the six years since Japanese aggression against China had begun in 1931, Tokyo's troops had conquered Chiang Kai-shek's capital at Nanking and forced the Nationalists to set up an exile government at Chunking and even forge a nervous alliance with the Communists to oppose the Japanese. At this point, Marshall was in no position to affect policy with regard to preparing for a two-theater (European and Asian) war, but, anticipating his eventual rise, he had already begun to think in terms of global strategy.

In December 1937, Douglas MacArthur resigned his commission and stepped down as army chief of staff to accept from Manuel L. Quezon, president of what was now the Commonwealth of the Philippines, semi-independent from the United States, an appointment as Quezon's military adviser with the lofty rank of field marshal of the Army of the Philippines.

His replacement as chief of staff was none other than General Malin Craig, the man who, thirty years earlier in Texas, had looked at Lieutenant George Marshall's disheveled uniform and found it impossible to believe he was an army officer. Things had changed. During the Great War, they had met again when Craig was on Hunter Liggett's staff, and they later served together on Pershing's staff. Craig was impressed with Marshall, and he had recently sat on the promotion board that had recommended him for his first star.

With Craig as the army's senior officer, Marshall had good reason to hope that he was finally in an advantageous position for rapid promotion. For now, however, he resumed inspections of the CCC camps of the Northwest. While conducting an inspection trip to Fort Missoula, Montana, during May 11–13, 1938, he received orders transferring him to the War Plans Division of the War Department in Washington, D.C., effective in July. Before leaving for this new desk assignment, he commanded the "Red Force" in joint Army–National Guard maneuvers. Major Mark Wayne Clark, an umpire in the maneuvers, praised Marshall's "imaginative" approach to a nighttime attack. Leaving what would be the last troop command of his career, Marshall at least had the satisfaction of departing on a high note.

⊢══⊣

As the Seventh Infantry and Vancouver High School bands played a farewell serenade for Brigadier General and Mrs. Marshall on their last night at Vancouver Barracks, armies in Asia, Europe, and Africa were either locked in battle or preparing for war. On that valedictory summer evening, the army of the United States of America was, by every measure, unready to march forth yet again to save the world for democracy.

As "Red Force" receded into memory, ahead of George Marshall lay the War Plans Division, a military universe on paper, in which battles were fought on maps, charts, and manpower graphs. He was again a staff officer, but this time with the promise that Malin Craig would retire soon and therefore Marshall had the prospect of following in the footsteps of his mentor and hero, Pershing, to the army's pinnacle, chief of staff, with four stars on his shoulders.

CHAPTER 7

Rainbow

"THANK GOD, GEORGE, YOU HAVE COME TO HOLD MY TREMBLING hands," General Malin Craig greeted Marshall when he reported to duty at the War Department on July 7, 1938.[1] Nearing retirement, Craig clearly wanted Marshall to succeed him. He was overwhelmed by the unpreparedness of the American war capability on the one hand and by the rapid expansion of the military on the other. The problem was that the need for expansion was urgent, and he needed to keep encouraging a sympathetic President Roosevelt to goad a reluctant Congress to speed up the expansion—and yet, the corps of staff officers as well as field officers was grossly insufficient to handle the expansion. Craig was like a man perishing from thirst, desperately demanding water, yet lacking an adequate vessel to hold it.

If Marshall needed compelling proof that he was finally being appreciated by the army, here it was—straight from the chief of staff, who believed that this brigadier general was the one man capable of resolving the preparedness paradox: the desperate and immediate need for more of everything, even though the army administration was already stretched beyond its capacity to manage the influx of resources. Craig wanted to give Marshall the leap in promotion he had so long craved. He wanted to jump him to deputy chief of staff. If this seemed to Craig just what was needed to steady his "trembling hands," such a promotion also presented a most thorny problem. As deputy, Marshall would suddenly find himself giving orders to nearly forty generals senior to him. Assuming they were good soldiers, those orders would be obeyed. But at what price in resentment and deterioration of morale at the very highest levels?

As if internal strife within the army staff hierarchy were not a sufficiently daunting prospect, Marshall was about to enter a bitter dispute between the advocates of the Army Air Corps, who believed that air power would determine the outcome of the next war, and the rest of the ground-based army. Also looming on the horizon was the navy, which competed with the army for precious defense dollars. Finally, there was the larger political situation. President Roosevelt both understood and advocated the need to get beyond the restrictions of the Neutrality Acts and move ahead on preparedness with all deliberate speed; however, there was still a powerful Republican isolationist, "America First" bloc to contend with, and FDR, always the consummate politician, knew that his task was to placate this wing without surrendering to it. FDR's selection of Harry Woodring as secretary of war, whose sentiments were in tune with the isolationists, was clearly intended as a nod to the America First faction; however, Louis Johnson, the influential *assistant* secretary of war, was an outspoken advocate of military expansion and preparedness. As army chief of staff, Malin Craig was squeezed between the two men—and so was Marshall. Fortunately, Woodring and Johnson did at least agree on Craig's choice of Marshall as his successor.

The autumn of 1938 brought the Sudetenland crisis in Europe, with Adolf Hitler threatening war unless Germany was permitted to annex the German-speaking portion of Czechoslovakia, the Sudetenland. The two principal democracies of Europe, France, and Britain, were bound by treaty to defend the integrity of the Czech nation, which had been created by the Treaty of Versailles after the World War. Britain's prime minister, Neville Chamberlain, flew to Munich to "appease" Hitler by giving him what he demanded in Czechoslovakia. Publicly, President Roosevelt greeted the apparent resolution of the crisis with relief, even as he confided to his cabinet that both England and France would soon have to wash the blood, Judas-fashion, from their hands. Chamberlain returned from Munich claiming to have brought with him "peace for our time," but the crisis set off a worldwide mania for rearmament.

Roosevelt responded by announcing to the press his intention to ask Congress for an additional half-billion dollars in defense funds. He also announced almost casually that he wanted the United States to produce 15,000 military aircraft annually. This created the context for Marshall's first meeting with the president, on November 14, 1938, which introduced Roosevelt to the uncompromisingly frank officer Malin Craig had anointed as his successor (see Introduction). More importantly, it made dramatically clear to Marshall the first big problem he would face when he succeeded Craig.

Clearly, the president wanted to build the nation's military. Marshall needed to ensure that this willingness did not become a political football, but would result in the creation of an effective army. His chief priority was to mold the expanded army into a balanced force. Marshall favored the creation of a mighty air force, but not at the expense of a mighty ground force. In this, he confronted a problem that would become all too familiar to secretaries of defense and uniformed chiefs in the postwar world as well. As the technology of warfare grew by enormous strides, military planners would always face pressures to embrace the latest technology and doctrine at the expense of older ones. During the Cold War, the American military would remold itself into principally a strategic force with the mission of fighting a thermonuclear war against the Soviet Union. The result was neglect of conventional warfighting capability, the lack of which was sorely felt in the Vietnam War. Similarly, in more recent conflicts, from Bosnia to Iraq and Afghanistan, warfighters have had to contend with a desire among politicians to avoid casualties by committing minimal forces to ground action and relying instead on air power and on emerging unmanned aerial vehicle (UAV) technologies. In his aim to create and maintain a balance in military capability, George Marshall would prove to be a model for future military leaders.

Thanks in good measure to the impression he made on FDR confidant Harry L. Hopkins (the former administrator of the popular Works Progress Administration), Roosevelt accepted Malin Craig's recommendation that Marshall succeed him, and the president nominated him both for elevation to chief of staff and for promotion, over nearly forty seniors, from brigadier to major general and, concurrently, temporary four-star full general. Marshall became chief on July 1, 1939, and was sworn in as a full general on September 1, 1939—the very day that World War II began in Europe when Adolf Hitler's armies streamed across the Polish border.

As it stood on that day, the Regular Army numbered 189,000 officers and men. He set about growing the force while maintaining a balance among the infantry and the emerging armored branch as well as the already burgeoning Air Corps. While building the strength of the force was a major priority, it was not Marshall's top priority. Drawing on his Fort Benning experience, he put training out front and installed Brigadier General Lesley McNair, the forward-looking commandant of the Command and General Staff School at Fort Leavenworth and an old and trusted friend, to overhaul tactical training in order to prepare the army for the war of movement and maneuver he knew it would have to fight. As Marshall saw it, this was no longer a theoretical assumption. He—and the rest of the world—had witnessed the German blitzkrieg ("lightning war") in action against Poland. Air, armor, and infantry were perfectly coordinated in a devastating, high-speed invasion that swept aside all resistance. Marshall well knew that the United States Army was far from capable of either fighting such an attack or defending against one. He intended that McNair should lead a training revolution that would give the army this capability.

While he oversaw the growth of the army—it was the beneficiary of the first peacetime draft in U.S. history, brought into being by passage of the Selective Training and Service Act of 1940—and its training for the realities of a new kind of warfare, Marshall also worked with a staff he handpicked to prepare war plans to meet an array of contingencies.

The War Department had been working for twenty years on plans to fight in another world war—though the debut of blitzkrieg had rendered many of these instantly obsolete—and Marshall himself had been instrumental in ensuring that Japan be considered in all planning. By the time he succeeded Malin Craig, six plans existed for fighting a two-ocean war based on the assumption that Japan would ally itself with Germany and Italy. These were designated RED, ORANGE, BLACK, GREEN, PURPLE, and BLUE. Under Marshall's direction, the plans were culled, revised, and collated by the spring of 1940 into a single master plan aptly designated RAINBOW. Whereas the December 7, 1941, Japanese attack on Pearl Harbor would come as a shock to the American public, Roosevelt and his military planners had long expected entry into the war. RAINBOW, developed by the Marshall staff, anticipated that the United States would form an alliance with Great Britain against both Japan and Germany. It also identified Germany as the stronger foe and greater threat, designating that it was to be given priority in the prosecution of the war.

By the summer of 1941, the Roosevelt administration was fully on the same page with Marshall and his staff in having concluded that the United States' entry into the war was inevitable. When the president agreed to the top secret Atlantic Conference with Winston Churchill, to be held aboard a ship in Placentia Bay off the coast of Newfoundland in August 1941, he insisted that Marshall accompany him, along with Air Corps leader General Henry H. "Hap" Arnold, Chief of Naval Operations Admiral Harold R. Stark, and Atlantic Fleet Commander Admiral Ernest J. King.

While Roosevelt had been constrained by neutrality laws against providing direct military assistance to Britain, he had already given a series of speeches to make a case for American intervention and at the same time had done all he could legally to aid the British. The Neutrality Act of 1939 permitted arms sales to Britain (and other nations) on a cash-and-carry basis. In March 1941, at FDR's urging, Congress passed the momentous Lend-Lease Act, which empowered the president to aid any nation whose defense he deemed critical to that of the United States, without cash payment. At Placentia Bay, he and Churchill agreed that once the United States was in the war, the RAINBOW priority of defeating Germany first would be followed, and that the earliest date for an invasion of Europe through France would be sometime in 1943. Leading up to the invasion would be a buildup of U.S. troops in the United Kingdom, later code-named Operation Bolero. Beyond this, the Atlantic Conference produced the Atlantic Charter, a kind of rough blueprint for the grand alliance of World War II in which Britain and America agreed on a set of war aims. As for Marshall, he was able to meet and establish cordial relations with his counterpart in the United Kingdom, Sir John Dill, chief of Britain's Imperial General Staff.

When Marshall returned to Washington from the Atlantic Conference, the army that he commanded stood at just under 1.5 million men, having grown exponentially from the force of 189,000 that had existed before passage of the Selective Training and Service Act of 1940. Most of them, however, were draftees whose terms of service would soon begin to expire and federalized National Guard units whose members were also slated to soon return to civilian life. The prospect of losing large numbers of trained men was discouraging in itself, but also troubling were the disappointing results of maneuvers held in August to test the readiness of this force. At Marshall's direction, new, far larger, and far more comprehensive maneuvers were scheduled to begin in September 1941 in Louisiana and Texas. The biggest war game in the country's history (a record still unbroken), known as the Louisiana-Texas maneuvers, exposed further inadequacies, but they also identified and spotlighted two exceptional officers.

Praised by the press as the star of the mock war for his skillful use of armor, Major General George S. Patton Jr. declared, "If you could take these tanks through Louisiana, you could take them through hell." Here was a virtuoso leader of mobile warfare, a commander capable of crafting an *American* blitzkrieg. He was also a colorful figure whose exploits were tailor-made for the papers. Reporters delightedly wrote of a frustrated military policeman who was directing traffic at an intersection in a town north of DeRidder, Louisiana, and was unable to unsnarl the jam. Patton suddenly appeared and started "cussing and raising hell." As the traffic jam began unwinding, a priest who had been celebrating Mass emerged from his church and told Patton to "hush up." Apologizing, Patton saluted the priest and turned the traffic control back to the M.P. Unafraid to bend the rules in order to win a war, Patton personally purchased out of his own pocket all the gasoline along Highway 171 so that when a competing general brought his "Red" army across the Sabine River to invade his "Blue Army" territory, there was no gasoline to fuel his tanks and other vehicles.

If Patton was the dashing tactician, another officer, with a name some reporters found difficult to pronounce let alone remember, revealed himself as a star among the planners of the maneuvers. Colonel Dwight D. "Ike" Eisenhower converted his tent into a kind of resort for reporters covering the maneuvers, charming the newsmen with his warmth and friendliness. Readers of influential columnist and radio commentator Drew Pearson's "Washington Merry-Go-Round" were told that the credit for the planning of the war games belonged to Eisenhower.

Chief of Staff George Marshall pored over analyses of the maneuvers, identifying the many areas that cried out for improvement even as he singled out the top-performing officers, among them Patton and Eisenhower, whom he would tap for important commands. At the same time, he kept abreast of the wealth of intelligence flowing in from a top-secret operation called MAGIC, which had broken Japan's diplomatic and naval codes and was decrypting messages probably faster than the staff of Japanese embassy in Washington. Although American and Japanese diplomats had been engaged in peace negotiations in Washington, the MAGIC decrypts revealed an unmistakable drift toward war in Tokyo's intentions. At a White House meeting on the afternoon of November 26, 1941, the secretary of state, Cordell Hull, warned the president, Secretary of War Henry Stimson, Navy Secretary Frank Knox, Chief of Naval Operations Admiral Harold Stark, and George Marshall that the Japanese were already poised for attack. "These fellows mean to fight," he said to the service chiefs. "You will have to be prepared."[2]

Back in his office in the War Department, Marshall read a MAGIC intercept reporting the movement of a Japanese convoy south of the Chinese island of Formosa. Its destination was unknown, but it posed a threat to the British colony of Singapore and the Philippines. Later that afternoon, Marshall sent his Pacific commanders a warning: "Japanese future action unpredictable, but hostile action possible at any moment. If hostilities cannot, repeat cannot, be avoided, the United States desires that Japan commit the first overt act."[3]

At the State Department, Secretary Hull handed Japan's envoys a "Ten Point Plan" which included demands that Japan withdraw its forces from Indochina and China. On the assumption that there would be no Japanese attack prior to a reply to the Hull ultimatum, Roosevelt departed Washington for a belated Thanksgiving dinner with patients at the Infantile Paralysis Center he had organized at Warm Springs, Georgia. Because Katherine Marshall was recuperating in Florida from broken ribs she had sustained in a fall the month before, Marshall gave up tickets to the Army-Navy football game to be played in Philadelphia and headed south to visit her.

When he returned to Washington on November 24, Marshall met Admiral Stark, who showed him the latest warning he intended to send to his naval commanders at Pearl Harbor, Hawaii, and the Philippines. Marshall concurred with Stark's conclusion that a favorable outcome of negotiations with Japan was "very doubtful." He immediately cabled a coded message to Douglas MacArthur, whom President Roosevelt had recalled to U.S. Army active duty in July 1941. Based in the Philippines, MacArthur now commanded all U.S. forces in the Far East. Marshall advised him that there was "no improvement in the international situation," and he warned that the "danger period is the first ten days of December" because reinforcements, equipment, and more B–17 bombers could not reach him in quantity until after that time. Only after December 10 would MacArthur have sufficient resources to make a Japanese attack "extremely hazardous."[4]

Working round the clock in the basement of the Munitions Building, the MAGIC code-breakers translated messages sent throughout early December. The intercepted messages ordered Japanese diplomats around the world to commence destroying code machines and ciphers. As if this were not a sufficiently clear indication that Japan was planning to go to war, the MAGIC team intercepted a message to Tokyo from its ambassador in Berlin reporting that the German Foreign Minister urged Japan to strike against the Americans and the British, and pledged Germany to join the war immediately. Tokyo's response to its man in Berlin was that American-Japanese negotiations had "ruptured" and Hitler was to be informed that "the breaking out of this war may come quicker than anyone dreams."

Early on the afternoon of Saturday, December 6, Colonel Rufus Bratton, head of the Far East Section of Army Intelligence, delivered to Marshall, Hull, and Stimson decrypted copies of an intercepted message from Tokyo to its pair of negotiators in Washington advising that a reply to Hull's Ten Point Plan would be transmitted to them in fourteen parts, with the final portion to be sent on Sunday morning, December 7. Each part was intercepted and duly decrypted. The last was intercepted at the U.S. Navy's monitoring station in Bainbridge, Maryland, at 4:37 A.M. Decoded by 7:00 A.M., and translated two hours later, the final section instructed the two emissaries to deliver the entire response to Secretary Hull at 1:00 P.M. that day. Reading this, along with the first thirteen parts, Bratton was convinced that a Japanese attack on an American installation somewhere in the Pacific was imminent. Accordingly, he phoned Marshall's quarters at Fort Myer, only to be informed that the chief of staff was taking his customary Sunday morning horseback ride. When Marshall returned Bratton's call at half-past ten, the colonel said he had "a most important message" and offered to bring it to Fort Myer.

"No, don't bother to do that," Marshall said. "I am coming down to my office. You can give it to me then."[5]

An hour later, while Bratton stood by, Marshall sat at his desk and read the entire text of the long Japanese message. He digested the material and sent an advisory to all Pacific commanders, noting, "Just what significance the hour set [1:00 P.M.] may have we do not know, but be on the alert accordingly." Marshall handed the advisory to Bratton, who, at 11:50 A.M., carried the alert to the Message Center with orders to get it out "at once by the fastest safe means." When he asked how long it would take for delivery, he was told thirty or forty minutes.

It took longer. The U.S. Army commander at Fort Shafter, Honolulu, Lieutenant Walter Short, received it three minutes after one in the afternoon, Washington time—7:33 A.M. in Honolulu. Six minutes later, the first of two waves of Japanese dive bombers and torpedo bombers launched from aircraft carriers 650 miles west of the Hawaiian Islands had the U.S. Navy base and U.S. Army facilities at and around Pearl Harbor in their sights. Battleships and other vessels of the U.S. Pacific Fleet were neatly moored stem to stern, and U.S. Army Air Corps planes arrayed wingtip to wingtip. The troops were at Sunday morning breakfast or just finishing it.

CHAPTER 8

Lighting a Flame

AT THREE O'CLOCK WASHINGTON TIME, DECEMBER 7, 1941, CHIEF of Staff George C. Marshall was attending the first wartime session of President Franklin D. Roosevelt's War Cabinet. Admiral Harold Stark was relaying to those present the reports of the Pearl Harbor devastation as they came in. As it became clear that the capital ships of the Pacific Fleet had been decimated, Stark's agitation increased markedly. In contrast, Marshall maintained a professional calm as he reviewed troop dispositions for the president.

Marshall recognized his first task as coping with the fog of war. The very nature of his character equipped him for this. Where others became emotional, he became engaged—alert and focused, but always composed. Some soldiers feared war; others loved it. For Marshall, however, war was a set of problems, and the only way to solve problems was to *work* the problems, one by one. Now, the first step in working a problem was to cut through the rumor, confusion, and panic of Pearl Harbor by separating reliable from unreliable information. Once the facts were available, the problem could be worked, and if the problem could be worked, it could be solved.

At the same time, Marshall set about recruiting the help he needed to run a war. Over the next few days, he added a new dimension to his already formidable reputation for organization. He quickly revealed a positive genius for choosing men of the highest caliber and matching them to the very jobs for which they were best suited. Five days after the Japanese attack left the Pacific Fleet in ruins, Marshall made perhaps his most fateful choice. At Third Army headquarters in San Antonio, Texas, Brigadier General Dwight D. Eisenhower took a phone call from an old friend, Colonel Walter Bedell Smith, whom, like everyone else who knew him well, Ike called "Beetle." Now assistant to the chief of staff, Beetle told Eisenhower that Marshall wanted him "to hop a plane and get up here right away" to join the War Plans Division.

Like Marshall in World War I, Ike had hoped to get into this war as a troop commander, and he was disappointed by the prospect of yet another staff position. He wrote later that he felt "heavy-hearted" as he informed his wife, Mamie, of the news. He packed a bag, and "within an hour I was headed for the War Department." An hour after his arrival at Washington's Union Station on December 14, he had received from Marshall the job of writing a plan "to do our best" to assist MacArthur in the Philippines, blunt the Japanese in the Pacific, and "win this whole war."[1]

Without meaning to be facetious, Eisenhower replied: "Give me a few hours." The plan he produced provided bare-bones support to help the Far East and Pacific commanders hold as much of their own as possible until they could be sent reinforcements. It wasn't much, but it addressed everything that could be addressed, and Marshall was impressed. Thus began a partnership between a West Point graduate, Class of 1915, and the VMI graduate, Class of 1902, which would produce, as their mutual biographer Mark Perry wrote, "The greatest victory in the history of our nation."[2]

As the American people did their best to celebrate Christmas amid the shocking reality that the nation was now at war, the president of the United States startled the public by revealing that since December 22 he had been playing host at the White House to Winston Churchill. Arriving secretly after an eight-day trip for a series of war strategy meetings code-named ARCADIA, the prime minister charmed the members of Congress in a December 26 speech to a joint session by conjecturing that if his father had been American and his mother British, "instead of the other way around," he might have gotten to Congress "on his own."

Ike, who had been wrestling with fighting in the Pacific on less than a shoestring, attended many of the meetings of U.S. and British military and naval staffs. He was not impressed. "Talk, talk, talk," he griped, observing the presence of "a lot of amateur strategists on the job, and prima donnas everywhere."[3] As for Marshall, his main concern during the conference was to create a unified command in each theater of operations, starting with the forces in the Far East. This meant one supreme commander for all service branches—army, navy, air—for both the United States and Britain. His belief was that ultimate success in the war depended upon it. For he had seen, close up, the waste of time and effort that had been created when General Pershing had been forced to fend off the shortsighted demands of French and British high command in what now had to be called the *First* World War. This *Second* World War, much bigger, much more complex, could not be fought to victory unless the Allies were of one mind and one will. Marshall possessed the vision to understand this from the very start, and he had the determination to ensure that this vision would not be allowed to fade or suffer compromise. Historians would credit Eisenhower, as Supreme Allied Commander, Europe, with successfully enforcing unified command, but the idea, the vision, the initial order was George Marshall's. Faced with strong opposition from service commanders of both countries, he doggedly argued the concept with generals, admirals, Roosevelt, and Churchill. And he won.

Marshall would also prevail in presenting a concept for creation of a Combined Chiefs of Staff to conduct the war on behalf of an even larger group of associated powers, including the Soviet Union. In a speech delivered on New Year's Day 1942, President Roosevelt christened this alliance the "United Nations."

As the ARCADIA conference ended, however, the incoming news was uniformly bad. General MacArthur's defense of the Philippines had dwindled to a last-ditch stand on the tiny island of Corregidor in Manila Bay. On January 23, he radioed Marshall, "I intend to fight it out to complete destruction." On February 15, the British gave up the struggle to save Singapore, moving Churchill to lament "the greatest disaster to British arms which our history records." On March 11, by Roosevelt's direct order, MacArthur and his wife and young son were plucked off of Corregidor by a U.S. Navy PT boat and sped on a supremely hazardous voyage to Mindanao Island, the Philippines, where the small family boarded a B–17 for the flight south to Australia. On landing, he announced that he had "come through" the Japanese blockade, and he promised the people of the Philippines, "I shall return."

He uttered the pledge as the newly appointed commander of U.S. Army forces in the Pacific. Having agreed with Churchill that the war in the Pacific would be primarily American (with contributions from Australia and New Zealand), Roosevelt further agreed that the Mediterranean Theater of operations would fall under British command, and that the European Theater command would be shared by the British and Americans, with the British Isles as the staging area for a cross-Channel invasion on a date to be determined. This was all very much in line with the original RAINBOW plan Marshall and his staff had drawn up.

Marshall set about streamlining the organization of the U.S. Army to enable decisions to be made and implemented quickly. He realized that fighting a mobile war required not only aircraft and tanks, but an efficient administrative bureaucracy. Throughout its history, the U.S. Army had been notably deficient in creating an adequate level of staff officers—the "middle management" of a military force, which ensured that the strategy of high command reached and was effectively executed by the commanders in the field. Marshall saw the war as an immense multinational enterprise that, whatever else it required, required effective management, management that facilitated rather than impeded the translation of strategy into action. He intended to see to it that *this* war would not repeat the inadequate management of previous wars.

Marshall created management systems, beginning with his own office. He assigned his most trusted assistants to plow through every scrap of paper that came his way, digest the material, filter it, reduce it to summary form, then report it to him. Much as a corps commander avoids commanding divisions and regiments by ensuring that he has divisional and regimental commanders who can do the job, Marshall chose subordinates who could be trusted to know just what matters to pass up to him while taking care of others on their own.

At every level, the soldier is the army, and so Marshall focused on getting the best people moved up into the most important positions. Eisenhower had proved himself so thoroughly and so rapidly that, on February 6, 1942, Marshall promoted him to head of the War Plans Division, replacing General Leonard T. Gerow, who was given command of the newly forming Twenty-ninth Infantry Division. Ike would have gladly swapped places with Gerow to get the troop command, but Marshall knew where his greatest talent lay, and he put him to work there.

Civilians and other military amateurs see war as a great explosion. Marshall saw it as a chaos that could be forced to yield order. To do this, he understood the necessity of defining a set of tasks to be completed. The very first task he assigned to his new head of War Plans was to deliver a memorandum defining a strategy for winning a global war to be waged on the land, at sea, and in the air by a disparate group of allies under the collective name United Nations. Submitted on March 25, 1942, the memo defined the goals of protecting the American continent, maintaining the security of England, keeping Russia in the war as an active ally, and defending the Middle East, which controlled vast oil supplies and the strategically critical Suez Canal. Although the American public clamored for instant revenge against Japan, Eisenhower cleaved to the RAINBOW priorities and identified Germany as the principal target for the first Allied offensive. It would be attacked through Western Europe. Marshall endorsed the plan and presented it to President Roosevelt, who gave his approval on April 1.

A week later, Marshall and Harry Hopkins were in London for conferences with Churchill and the British high command to implement Operation Bolero, the buildup of U.S. forces in Great Britain. Among those with whom Marshall conferred was Lord Louis Mountbatten, head of Britain's Special Operations, popularly known as Commandos. Ordinarily, a chief of staff would not be expected to concern himself with small-unit special operations, not when vast armies had to be organized, deployed, supplied, and furnished with commanders. But, as usual, Marshall was not committed to what was expected, but to what had the best chance of doing some good. Even moving ahead at full speed, he knew that creating adequate forces to fight a two-front war would take time. Commando units offered the prospect of mounting truly effective operations sooner rather than later and, even more important, they afforded American soldiers and officers the opportunity of combat experience—again, soon. America's warriors would arrive at the front well trained, Marshall believed, but he also knew that the best training came on the job, in combat. The Commando concept was a means of creating seasoned fighting men who could then be assigned to larger incoming units, which would thereby have the benefit of their experience. When he left London, special ops were very much on his mind.

Back in Washington, Marshall consulted his famous little black book, the list he had long kept and maintained of promising officers. In need of someone to follow up on his visit to London, he selected Colonel Lucian King Truscott Jr. Born in Texas, Truscott grew up in the Oklahoma territory and graduated from a Reserve Officers' training school in 1917. After cavalry service on the Mexican border during World War I, he chose to make the army his career. Truscott attended all of the service schools, meeting Marshall and Eisenhower along the way, and distinguished himself in the Louisiana-Texas maneuvers. When Truscott arrived at the Operations Division, Ike explained to him that General Marshall had arranged with Mountbatten to send a group of American officers to England for assignment to Britain's Combined Operations Headquarters. Their purpose was to plan for training Americans in the hit-and-run-tactics of Britain's Commandos. Truscott would command these men.

After reviewing British documents and conferring with others assigned to the mission, Truscott met with General Marshall, the man who had given him the job.

"His calm and dignified personality was most impressive," Truscott later wrote. "He shook my hand in a quick firm grasp, indicating a chair beside him. Leaning back slightly in his own chair, he gazed at me steadily."

Without a change in expression, Marshall said slowly, "You are an older man than I wanted for this assignment. I looked you up. You are forty-seven. Mountbatten is forty-three. Most of his staff are younger. All of them are battle-experienced. They are even now engaged in planning and conducting raids against the Germans."

Truscott could think of nothing to say. This was just as well, he later wrote, because his mouth was too dry for him to speak in any case.

Marshall continued: "Some of your friends assure me that you are younger than your years, and that your experience especially fits you for this assignment."

When Truscott attempted to explain his *lack* of qualifications, Marshall disregarded him and went on to describe Mountbatten, the organization he headed, the activities in which they were currently engaged, and the part they would have in making preparations for the projected invasion. He expressed concern because Americans would be committed to their first battle. He had no fear that they would be inadequately trained, but he knew that only actual battle could fully prepare men psychologically to meet the anxieties and uncertainties of combat. In World War I, American forces had been "blooded"—exposed to combat—in relatively quiet sectors of the Western Front before being fully committed to battle. The nature of the proposed operations in this new war precluded any large-scale "blooding" of U.S. divisions, as was the case in World War I, but it was still possible to provide combat experience to the small number of men who participated in Commando raids. Some of these experienced men would then be assigned to every subsequent assault unit, so that each green outfit would have the benefit of some combat veterans, whose presence might counter the bad effects of fearful imagination and panicky rumor always associated with inexperience. The Commandos would be equipped to disseminate practical information among their comrades.

This, Marshall explained, was the main reason he had arranged with Lord Mountbatten to send Truscott's group to London. Small-unit Commando assaults were the quickest way to get Americans into combat productively and were therefore the most effective way to instill combat experience into the American army. The small force of Commandos would, in a manner of speaking, instill combat readiness among the much larger forces of the American army as a whole.

It was a brilliant insight and an extraordinarily innovative approach to building a battle-seasoned army from scratch.

Marshall's plan was to conduct increasingly ambitious raids against the German-held continent until the time for the invasion in 1943. As many American soldiers as possible would be given an opportunity to participate in these operations. Marshall was in the business of creating veterans, and Truscott's task would be to arrange for this participation and to ensure the efficient dissemination of this battle experience among assault units. He would work with members of Mountbatten's staff and would assist in every way possible in the training of American troops and the preparations for the invasion.

"This interview made an everlasting impression upon me," Truscott wrote. "General Marshall had removed any confusion in my mind as to what was expected of me. For the rest, it was up to me."[4] In this sentence, Truscott distilled what might be called the "Marshall effect." Whatever the identity of the enemy in the field, for Marshall, the deadliest foe was confusion; therefore, the first objective was to defeat it. That done—and it was invariably done—expectation suddenly became wondrously clear, and those who answered to Marshall knew what they had to do. It became their responsibility to do it.

+⟩══⟨+

After hastily made travel arrangements and a week-long journey that included a transatlantic flight plagued by stormy winter weather, Truscott and his team arrived in bleak, bomb-shattered London on May 17, 1942. Lord Mountbatten informed him that the Combined Operations Command had been organized from personnel of the three services and that it would have an important part in planning, training for, and carrying out the invasion. Truscott found Combined Operations Headquarters (COHQ) to be like no other headquarters he had known. Not only were British staff organization and procedures different from those in the U.S. Army, but there were differences resulting from combining three services in a single staff, and others resulting from the personality of the man who was Chief of Combined Operations. A few weeks elapsed before the Americans became so familiar with the organization and procedures that they felt they could go about their work with confidence. Nine days after setting foot in England, Truscott griped in a letter to his wife, Sarah, "Everything is done by committee."[5]

Recognizing that American soldiers were to be transported in British craft and supported by Royal Navy elements, operating under control of COHQ, Truscott decided that it was logical to form a purely American unit. Consequently, on May 26, 1942, he sent Marshall a proposal that he be permitted to base the training on the Commando concept, but adapted to U.S. Army tables of organization and equipment. Marshall cabled his approval two days later. Truscott next dealt with Eisenhower's special requirement that the U.S. Commandos be given a uniquely American name. While several appellations were proposed in discussions with aides, Truscott found the solution to the dilemma in a band of irregular fighters during the French and Indian War. Formed by Major Robert Rogers and known as "Rogers' Rangers," they had moved from the annals of history into American popular culture in 1937 via Kenneth Roberts's novel *Northwest Passage* and a 1940 movie of the same name based upon it. Thus the U.S. Army's "First Ranger Battalion" was created. General Russell Hartle, commanding officer of the Thirty-fourth Division, headquartered in Northern Ireland, was authorized to choose the battalion's commander. He selected a young West Pointer who had been one of his aides since the division had arrived in Northern Ireland a few months earlier.

Thirty-three year-old William Orlando Darby had been born and raised in Fort Smith, Arkansas, and had graduated from West Point in 1933. As an artillery officer, he had gained experience in conducting amphibious assaults during a week of combined operations in training exercises in Puerto Rico. Hoping to be put in command of a combat outfit in the Pacific, he had been frustrated and outspoken about his dismay at being assigned to an administrative post as Hartle's aide in Northern Ireland. He jumped at the chance to set up, train, and lead the battalion, which, as "Darby's Rangers," was destined to become one of the most storied outfits of World War II.

+=====+

As Marshall had sent Truscott to England to implement his vision of a Commando force as an incubator for a combat-seasoned, battle-ready American army, so he next dispatched Eisenhower, together with Army Air Corps chief "Hap" Arnold and Mark Wayne Clark, chief of staff to U.S. ground forces commander Leslie McNair, to ensure that all London-based senior American officers were thoroughly indoctrinated in the objectives of the War Department. Unity of command, Marshall reasoned, must begin with a seamless understanding between field commanders and those at the highest levels. War was inherently the enemy of understanding. Marshall intended for understanding to prevail. Between him and Eisenhower there was near-perfect understanding, but when Ike examined James E. Chaney, Commanding General, European Theater of Operations (ETO), he concluded that the man had no understanding of his role and should be sent home "on a slow boat, without escort."[6] There was no room for weak links at the top.

On June 8, 1942, Eisenhower drew up a detailed report to Marshall on the situation in the ETO, in which he recommended replacing Chaney with an individual who was "thoroughly indoctrinated in the plans of the United States Government, with a working knowledge of our capabilities in the production of land, air, and naval units and materials to support them in offensive fighting." He appealed to the chief of staff that this report was one paper he should make a point to read in detail because "it was likely to be an important document in the further waging of the war."

"I certainly do want to read it," Marshall replied. "You may be the man who executes it. If that's the case, when can you leave?"[7]

Dwight D. Eisenhower's appointment as the U.S. commanding general in the ETO was officially announced on June 11, 1942. Ike noted in his war memoir that when he arrived in London to run "the whole shebang," the United States was just hitting its stride in the mobilization and training of its armies, navies, and air forces. Only the Thirty-fourth Division, the First Armored Division, and a few small detachments of the U.S. Army Air Forces had arrived in Northern Ireland, about 30,000 men in all, and most of them only partly trained. The great bulk of the equipment needed for an invasion of the European continent not only had not arrived, it did not yet exist. Some landing craft had yet to enter the blueprint stage.

The importance of invading Europe as soon as possible was to open up a Western Front to take pressure off the Soviets on the Eastern Front. However, it soon become clear that this invasion, slated for 1943, could not take place until early 1944. Leaders in Washington and London therefore began considering alternative ways to relieve the pressure on the Soviet Union and also to meet President Roosevelt's demand that the U.S. forces engage the Germans as early as possible. Churchill proposed an invasion of French Morocco, Algeria, and Tunisia to trap Field Marshal Erwin Rommel's vaunted Afrika Korps between Anglo-American forces in the west and the British Eighth Army in Egypt. Insisting that U.S. ground troops be put into action against the enemy in 1942, Roosevelt approved a North Africa invasion plan in July, and in early August, American and British officers met to begin planning Operation Torch. Marshall, as we will see in Chapter 9, reluctantly approved and, insisting on the unified command approach, specified that Eisenhower have overall command of British as well as American forces.

On September 5, 1942, the Allies agreed that landings would be made by Anglo-American forces sailing from Great Britain and targeting the coastal cities of Algiers and Oran in Algeria. Marshall insisted that, simultaneously, U.S. forces should sail from the United States to land principally at Casablanca in Morocco. Algiers and Oran were on the Mediterranean, east of the Strait of Gibraltar. Marshall believed that it was essential to land a substantial force west of the strait as well. If fascist-ruled Spain suddenly decided to join the war on the side of Germany and Italy, it was vital to maintain an overland line of communication with the landing forces in Algiers. To lead the Western Task Force, as the Casablanca-bound unit was designated, Marshall heartily approved the selection of George S. Patton Jr. Thus the U.S. Army would enter World War II with the man who would prove to be among its best and most difficult field commanders.

Left to right, Colonel Campbell King; Brigadier General John Leonard Hines, commander 1st Brigade, 1st Division; and Lt. Colonel George C. Marshall, France 1918. (George C. Marshall file, Personalities collection). Photo Credit: USAMHI

Colonel George C. Marshall with Major General Henry T. Allen in 1918. Photo Credit: USAMHI (George C. Marshall file, Personalities collection)

General George C. Marshall, chief of staff. Photo courtesy of the Library of Congress

Marshall, left, as Army Chief of Staff, testified before the House Appropriations Subcommittee on November 27, 1940 in support of President Roosevelt's request for $271,999,523 to finance national defense deficiencies. He is shown with Rep. Edward T. Taylor, Colo., Chairman of the Committee. The military was so unpopular with an isolationist public at this time that Marshall chose to appear in civilian clothing. Photo courtesy of the Library of Congress

General Hsiung of the Chinese army visits Marshall in Washington, 1942. Photo courtesy of the Library of Congress

While attending the Casablanca Conference in January 1943, President Roosevelt, with Major General George S. Patton, Jr. (right), presents the Medal of Honor to Brig. General William H. Wilbur as General George C. Marshall looks on. Photo courtesy of the Library of Congress

Teheran, Iran. Dec. 1943. Standing outside the Russian Embassy, left to right: Unidentified British officer, General George C. Marshall, shaking hands with Sir Archibald Clark Keer, British Ambassador to the USSR, Harry Hopkins, Marshal Stalin's interpreter, Marshal Josef Stalin, Foreign minister Molotov, General Voroshilov. Picture was taken during the Teheran conference. Photo courtesy of the Library of Congress

April 2, 1951. President Harry Truman signs a proclamation making May 19 Armed Forces Day. At the time of this photograph, the army had been operating the nation's railroads for over seven months during a labor strike of unprecedented scope and duration. Secretary of Defense Marshall is seated beside the president, and Secretary of the Army Frank Pace, Jr., stands between the seated men. Photo Credit: USAMHI (George C. Marshall file, Personalities collection)

CHAPTER 9

Blood and Sand

Since Sunday, December 7, 1941, life for Katherine Marshall had been marked by her husband's long absences, dinners interrupted or canceled, phone calls in the middle of the night, and increasing worries about the effect of stress on his health. After nearly three years in residence in Quarters No. 1 at Fort Myer, they bought a country house called Dodona Manor in Leesburg, Virginia, but it was not until Marshall returned from his fist visit to wartime London that she was able to show him the work she had overseen to get it ready for them to live in. Situated in the Blue Ridge Mountain foothills, thirty-five miles from Washington, it had been built in 1786 by a nephew of George Washington and had ample space for gardening, one of Marshall's great pleasures. "This is home," he declared, "a real home after forty-one years of wandering."

When complimentary box-seat tickets arrived at Dodona Manor for the Washington Redskins nighttime football game at Griffith Stadium on November 8, 1942, Katherine saw an opportunity for her husband to escape his job for a few hours. When he told her he "could not be out of touch with the office," she invited General and Mrs. Henry "Hap" Arnold to go to the game with her instead. The crowd recognized the chief of the Army Air Forces, and a great cheer went up. Wishing her husband had come with her, she fretted and paid little attention to the action on the gridiron. Presently, a voice boomed from the loudspeakers: "Stop the game! Important announcement! The President of the United States announces the successful landing on the African Coast of an American Expeditionary Force. This is our Second Front."[1]

Patton's Western Task Force, consisting of 35,000 men, had succeeded in taking its assigned objectives in French Morocco, Casablanca and a key airfield at Port-Lyautey. (Since its defeat in the summer of 1940, France had been divided into a large occupied zone and a smaller unoccupied zone, which, however, was only nominally self-governing. Vichy France, as this collaborationist entity was called, extended to the French colonies in North Africa and was obligated by the terms of the armistice with Germany to cooperate with German forces in resisting the Allied invasion; however, the allegiance of the Vichy colonial civil and military leaders was a highly fluid matter; very few were enthusiastic Nazi collaborators.)

Central Task Force, commanded by U.S. Major General Lloyd R. Fredendall, consisted of 18,500 U.S. Army troops with the mission of capturing Oran in Algeria. Among the men who hit the beaches were Darby's Rangers. Tasked with spearheading a pair of landings at the port of Arzew, Algeria, they knocked out two large coastal artillery installations to clear the way for troops led ashore by Major General Terry de la Mesa Allen, while his deputy, Major General Theodore (Ted) Roosevelt Jr., led the landing at Oran.

Eastern Task Force, under British Lieutenant General Kenneth A. N. Anderson, included 20,000 troops in the first wave, half of them American and half British. Their objective was the city of Algiers.

Operation Torch, the North African landings, was not what Marshall had wanted. He had assigned Eisenhower to plan Operation Sledgehammer, a limited invasion of France from England via the English Channel. Churchill and the British high command had objected, arguing that such an invasion was premature, whereas Roosevelt insisted only that, one way or another, American troops get into combat as soon as possible, though he did most favor Churchill's idea of invading North Africa. Both Marshall and Eisenhower saw this as a long diversion from making a more immediately effective assault on Europe itself, but Marshall could not prevail against the combined forces of Churchill and his own president. Marshall warned that focusing on North Africa now would not only prevent Operation Sledgehammer from going ahead, but would also delay what was at the time called Operation Roundup, the larger cross-Channel invasion of Europe that had been set for 1943. The British War Cabinet at first refused to accept such a postponement and wanted all mention of it removed from Marshall's memorandum regarding the North African invasion; Churchill and his advisers did not want to admit—especially to the beleaguered Soviet Union's Joseph Stalin, impatient for the Allies to open up a western front—that the North African operation was bound to delay the Allied liberation of continental Europe. At this, Marshall dug in his heels, warning the British that if the wording was not included, he would refuse to go along with the North African operation. At the insistence of Britain's Field Marshal Sir Alan Brooke, who had championed the North African assault, the War Cabinet accepted Marshall's warning and included it in the proposal. With this caveat, Operation Torch went ahead.

Marshall approved the final plan for Torch, and operational orders were issued between October 3 and 20, 1942, in eight parts. They outlined the strategic plan, routing and scheduling of the three convoys, instructions for landings, descriptions of submarine screens to cover the assaults, and convoy arrangements for the period after the landings. The last of the task forces was due at Gibraltar on November 4.

Opposing the landings would be Vichy French forces with an estimated strength of 120,000, mostly native rank-and-file with French officers, supported by 500 aircraft and a sizable fleet at Toulon. The Italian fleet also presented a threat, but it suffered from low morale, poor leadership, and a shortage of fuel oil. The most serious challenge was the German Luftwaffe based in Italy and North Africa. While planners hoped that the French would offer only token resistance to satisfy the demands of "French honor," Marshall insisted that plans be based on the worst-case assumption that the French might bitterly resent being attacked because they were deemed to be allied with Germany and would therefore offer serious resistance. Marshall approved a secret mission to persuade the French authorities in Morocco and Algeria to cooperate in the invasion, and the dashing American Major General Mark Clark—Churchill called the tall man with the beaklike nose "my American eagle"—slipped into Algeria aboard the British submarine *Seraph* and successfully negotiated French compliance with the invasion. In a related effort to pacify the Vichy French, Eisenhower met at Gibraltar with French general Henri Giraud, who agreed to cooperate with the Allied invasion, although he was disappointed at Eisenhower's refusal to put him in charge of it. The plan also called upon the chief American diplomat in Morocco, Robert Murphy, to cajole French officials in Casablanca to refrain from resisting the invasion, and Eisenhower subsequently also co-opted General Alphonse Juin, French army commander in chief in North Africa, and Admiral François Darlan, a major figure in the Vichy colonial administration.

+=====+

In the U.S. Army's first invasion of the war, the soldiers of Patton and Truscott traveled farther than any other invasion force of World War II. The journey to Morocco across the Atlantic that started on October 23 took almost two weeks. On October 20, 1942, Eisenhower wrote to Marshall, "If a man permitted himself to do so, he could get absolutely frantic about questions of weather, politics, personalities in France and Morocco, and so on. To a certain extent, a man must merely believe in his luck and figure that a certain amount of good fortune will bless us when the critical day arrives."[2]

After setting up headquarters at Gibraltar, Ike mused in a message to Marshall on the day before the landings, "We are standing, of course, on the brink and must take the jump—whether the bottom contains a nice feather bed or a pile of brickbats."[3]

For Eisenhower, the invasion was his first venture in commanding troops in combat. For Franklin D. Roosevelt, the objective of the landings in North Africa had been as much political as military, answering the desire of the American people to take the war to the Germans and meeting the demand by Soviet Premier Joseph Stalin for a second front. For Marshall, Operation Torch was the culmination of years of developing the doctrine of mobile war and of advocating his concept of unified command. To focus attention on the vindication of his efforts to turn the unified command idea into reality, he accepted an invitation to address a meeting of the Academy of Political Science at the Astor Hotel in New York on November 10, 1942.

"In the past two days," he said, "we have had a most impressive example of the unity of command, an American Expeditionary Force, soldiers, sailors, and aviators, supported by the British Fleet, by British flyers and by a British Army, all controlled by an American commander in chief, General Eisenhower, with a Deputy Commander also an American officer, General Clark. They are served by a combined staff of British and American officers, of soldiers, sailors, and aviators. Officers of the British Army and Navy senior to General Eisenhower, men of great distinction and long experience, have, with complete loyalty, subordinated themselves to his leadership."[4]

The North African Campaign would never go smoothly, but, from early on, it was clear that the Allies would not be pushed back into the sea, and President Roosevelt was right in quickly calling Operation Torch a turning point of the war. From new War Department headquarters in a sprawling, five-sided building on the Virginia side of the Potomac River—the largest office building in the world—Marshall sent a Christmas gift of a fifty-inch globe to Winston Churchill. Noting in a letter that the skies had cleared considerably since "those dark weeks when you and your chiefs first met with us a year ago," and that "the enemy faces our powerful companionship in arms which dooms his hopes and guarantees our victory," he could point out on the globe that Americans had stopped the Japanese advances in the Pacific with stunning victories over the Japanese fleet at Midway and in the Coral and Bismarck Seas. U.S. Marines had taken the offensive at Guadalcanal in the Solomon Islands. Air assaults on Germany and northwestern Europe by the Royal Air Force and the U.S. Eighth Air Force out of the United Kingdom had grown heavier and heavier. In the Soviet Union, the Red Army had broken the siege at Stalingrad and encircled the German Sixth Army, opening the way for a Soviet offensive. Since Pearl Harbor, the strength of the U.S. Army had skyrocketed from a million and a half men in 37 divisions to five and one-third million in 73 divisions, with one-fifth of that strength located overseas. This growth and deployment had all been managed on Marshall's watch and owed a great deal to his genius at organization and mobilization. The key was his extensive experience in both logistics and training, two functions he integrated in the mobilization. This ensured a steady flow of men from induction through deployment, the likes of which had not been seen in World War I.

On December 31, 1942, Marshall's staff arranged a surprise party to mark his sixty-second birthday. With everyone raising a glass of sherry in salute, Secretary of War Henry Stimson hailed Marshall as one of the most selfless public officials he had ever known. Six weeks earlier, when it was clear that the Allies were ashore in North Africa to stay, he had credited Marshall as the author of the most difficult and complex expeditionary plan that the United States had ever tackled. Marshall had replied that he thought they had better wait and see how things went. At the time of the birthday party, a successful outcome of Operation Torch's objective of driving the Germans out of North Africa still remained in doubt.

General Eisenhower was disappointed that the Germans had interrupted the Allied drive into Tunisia before it reached and captured Tunis, a key port. Throughout much of December, British general Harold R. I. G. Alexander tried to renew the Allied effort to attain this objective, but was repeatedly thwarted by bad weather. Although Ike was vocal about his dismay, after a trip to the front at the end of December, he decided to postpone resumption of the drive against Tunisia until the weather was more favorable. At this time, he also discussed with the commanders in the field the feasibility and advisability of commencing an operation farther south, where the terrain was more accommodating and the climate drier. His idea was to use the U.S. First Armored Division and a regimental combat team of the First Infantry Division to sever the German lines of communication with Tunis. This would leave the town ripe for the taking.

Studies by Eisenhower's staff suggested that the plan was workable and that the necessary forces could be assembled in and around Tébessa, Algeria, by January 22. The British First Army had been designated to control all operations in Tunisia. When the French occupying a wide sector of the front refused to serve under British command, Eisenhower assumed operational control of all Allied forces; the French had no objection to working under U.S. command. His intention was to create under his deputy chief of staff Lucian Truscott a small command group near the headquarters of First Army at Constantine.

Marshall had done a thorough job of indoctrinating Eisenhower in the paramount importance of unified command, and, from the beginning, Eisenhower was determined to apply the concept unrelentingly. The idea was Marshall's, but its faithful execution belonged to Eisenhower and was carried out, more often than not, amid continual griping from both American and British field commanders. Marshall and Eisenhower were unshakably convinced that unified command—the absolute authority of a single supreme commander pledged to act without regard to national allegiance—was the very foundation of a successful Anglo-American alliance. Ike understood, however, that it was dangerous to push unified command down into the British field echelons because this gave the appearance of violating the chain of command by intruding American authority between senior and subordinate British officers. But rather than see the advance on Tunis fail because of French hard feelings toward the British, he decided to take the risk.

Eisenhower's immediate objective was to clear the Germans and their Italian allies from Tunisia and capture the port of Tunis. His forces had taken defensive positions in mountains between the Mediterranean Sea on the north and the Sahara Desert on the south. Moving east into Tunisia as the Germans moved west, they would face the enemy on a curving front, from Medjez-el-Bab in the north to El Guettar in the south, called the Mareth Line. With Italians operating in the fore, and Colonel-General Hans-Jürgen von Arnim's Fifth Panzer Army poised near Tunis, the Panzer Army Africa stood ready to rush from Libya under the command of Erwin Rommel.

Headquarters of the U.S. II Corps under Major General Lloyd Fredendall was at Tébessa in a region called Speedy Valley located west of the Grand Dorsal mountain range. With the bulk of his troops committed to protection of lines of communication, Eisenhower had decided to detach II Corps, of which the First Armored Division was the nucleus, from the Center Task Force at Oran in order to concentrate it in Tunisia. On January 1, 1943, he appointed Fredendall to command II Corps, including a French force at Constantine and a British paratroop brigade. He was to concentrate these forces in the Tébessa and Kasserine area to prepare for an offensive action against the enemy's lines of communication. Having completed this concentration in mid-January, II Corps was to be ready to launch an attack by January 23. Success depended on perfect coordination with the British to contain Arnim's forces.

Before II Corps arrived in the south in late December 1942, Ike learned that Rommel had correctly analyzed the strategic situation. Although his force was in full retreat from the British Eighth Army, in a captured document dated December 16, 1942, Rommel posited that the Allies suffered from weaknesses inherent in a combined command and proposed to hold the British Eighth Army with a minimum force and use the remainder to attack and cut off Allied lines of communication in Tunisia. Calculating that two divisions could either hold the Eighth Army or delay its pursuit of the German withdrawal, he proposed to advance the bulk of his force against vulnerable Allied lines of communication in the south. Arnim's mission would be to keep a corridor open for Rommel's advance northward from Libya along the coast of the Gulf of Gabès to link up with Arnim's Panzer Army and form a front from which would be pushed westward to keep the Allies from taking both Tunis and the port of Bizerte.

Arriving at Constantine on January 2, 1943, with a bad cold, Lucian Truscott was assigned as his first task in an operation against Rommel (codenamed SATIN) to find an advanced command post for Eisenhower that was closer to the front than Algiers. He selected an almost empty orphanage in Constantine as a suitable location for the command post. It had a villa next door that was deemed suitable as quarters for Eisenhower. On January 14, the post was open for business. During the second week of the month, there were conferences between various staff sections dealing with organization of the advanced command post (CP) and SATIN planners.

Before settling into his headquarters at the front, Eisenhower found himself sidetracked by the momentous Casablanca Conference between Roosevelt and Churchill at the hotel Anfa in Casablanca on January 14. The two leaders had made a point of convening close to the front as if to demonstrate their complete confidence that North Africa was on the verge of conquest. Marshall was in attendance, as were members of British high command. While FDR and Churchill agreed on overall war aims, Marshall and Eisenhower hammered out with their British counterparts the military aspects of a strategy for winning a world war. They reaffirmed their resolve to concentrate efforts against Germany in the hopes of drawing German forces away from the Eastern Front, and to increase shipments of supplies to the Soviet Union. While they would begin concentrating forces in England in preparation for an eventual landing in northern France, Marshall bowed to the prevailing will of the British and the political will of FDR in agreeing to concentrate first on the Mediterranean, what Churchill called "the soft underbelly of Europe," by jumping off from North Africa (after the Axis was cleared out of it) to invade Sicily, from which the next step was the Italian mainland. This would knock

Italy out of the war. Marshall and the others also agreed to strengthen the strategic bombing campaign against Germany—a controversial step, as Marshall and the other ground-oriented planners were not entirely persuaded of the effectiveness of strategic bombing.

On the final day of the Casablanca Conference, President Roosevelt announced that he and Churchill had decided (with Stalin concurring in absentia) that the only way to ensure postwar peace was to adopt a policy of absolute victory—that is, the unconditional surrender of all Axis powers. Roosevelt said he wanted to avoid the situation that had followed World War I, when large segments of German society supported the position, so deftly exploited by the Nazi party, that Germany had not been defeated militarily, but had been "stabbed in the back" by liberals, pacifists, socialists, communists, and Jews. Roosevelt also wished to make it clear that neither the United States nor Great Britain would seek a separate peace with the Axis powers. (Again, Stalin agreed in absentia.)

Calling Churchill as alternately defiant and jocular, *New York Times* correspondent Drew Middleton wrote, "He described General Field Marshal Erwin Rommel as a fugitive from Libya and Egypt now trying to pass himself off as the liberator of Tunis. But he reminded the correspondents that General Sir Bernard L. Montgomery was hot on Marshal Rommel's trail and that everywhere that Mary went the lamb was sure to go."[5] Like other top U.S. commanders, Marshall was concerned that the high profile the press was giving "Monty" not only damaged the morale of the U.S. Army, but, more important, undermined unified command. Believing that because Eisenhower had only three-star lieutenant general rank as the Allied commander in chief in North Africa the general was at a disadvantage when dealing with four-star British officers *under* him, Marshall urged Roosevelt to promote Ike to full general. Roosevelt demurred. While Eisenhower had done a good job, said the president, "he still hasn't knocked the Germans out of Tunisia."[6] Traveling with Eisenhower to his headquarters in Algiers, Marshall promised Ike he would soon get four stars.

Marshall was always careful to avoid encroaching on areas he believed to be the sole responsibility of his field commanders; however, he shared two concerns with Eisenhower, based on what he had seen in North Africa. The first was his sense that U.S. battlefield commanders were insufficiently aggressive and lacking in drive. The second was his perception that Ike spent too much time in the field, his implication being that he was trying to do the job of his battlefield commanders. As a way of addressing both of his concerns, Marshall gave Ike a piece of unconventional advice, suggesting that he take on a roving deputy with enough rank to go into any headquarters and bring back information that could be trusted. It was a most delicate idea, since any such "deputy" might well be perceived by field commanders as Ike's spy, suggesting that the supreme commander did not trust them. But the theater was so far-flung and the problems presented by trying to maintain unified command so complex that Marshall strongly believed that only a high-ranking deputy, on the scene, could deliver Eisenhower the accurate picture of the situation he required. Marshall, whose ability to put the right man in the right job was already legendary, suggested that Eisenhower appoint Major General Omar N. Bradley.

It was not, on the face of it, an obvious choice. At the time in command of the Twenty-eighth Division in Florida, Bradley had been Ike's classmate at West Point in the class of 1915, but, in the postwar retrospect of his memoir, *Crusade in Europe,* Ike wrote: "He was especially suited to act in such an intimate capacity, not only by reason of our long friendship, but because of his ability and reputation as a sound, painstaking, and broadly educated soldier."[7]

Much of that broad education had come directly from Marshall at Fort Benning. Not only was Marshall impressed by Bradley's ability to see beyond outworn military convention to assess a particular situation, but he also knew him to be an unpretentious soldier, an egoless team player. What is more, Marshall knew that others saw him this way. They might think of him as Ike's spy, but at least they would know that he had no personal axe to grind.

While Marshall made the long, circuitous flight back to Washington, Eisenhower faced a new challenge on the Tunisian battlefield. With Rommel retreating westward from Libya into Tunisia and with Montgomery's British Eighth Army in hot pursuit, the U.S. right flank, held by II Corps under Lloyd Fredendall, was suddenly in peril. Fredendall's plan was to strike eastward from the Feriana-Gafsa area with the First Armored Division and one Regimental Combat Team of the First Infantry Division. They would seize a bottleneck in Rommel's line of communications at Gabès on the eastern coast of Tunisia. With minefields laid to protect the U.S. right flank against any reaction by Rommel, Fredendall planned to swing north to capture the town of Sfax. These operations would be supported by U.S. tactical aviation operating from airfields at Tébessa, Feriana, Thelepte, and elsewhere in Algeria and Tunisia.

Fredendall, who hoped to achieve all this in about ten days, set January 30 as D-Day for the offensive to step off. Until it did, however, the main force opposing the Germans would be the French, who, under the circumstances, proved, as expected, unreliable. On January 17, the French commander reported that the Germans were attacking his position at Pont du Fahs, just beyond the British sector. After an urgent conference with British Lieutenant General Kenneth Anderson, Truscott, ever the realist, agreed with Anderson that the French could never contain the situation on their own. In fact, the surprise German attack at Pont du Fahs set off a sequence of events with unanticipated consequences in unexpected places. The result was that the Germans, for a very anxious time, wrested the initiative and the momentum from the Allies.

From Tébessa, one of the main roads leading toward Sfax on the Tunisian plain passed through the easternmost mountain chain at the village of Faid and a vital pass that was essential for any Allied advance toward German lines of communication at Sfax. In German hands it would expose the forward airfields at Feriana and Thelepte to attack by German ground forces and facilitate a German advance toward Tébessa and to the northwest. When the French were attacked at Faid Pass on January 28, General Anderson ordered Fredendall to restore the situation. As German forces cut off and overwhelmed two battalions of American infantry placed too far apart for mutual support, and as Panzers reversed attacks by U.S. reserves, including elements of the First Armored Division, the Americans evacuated airfields and supply depots on the plain and withdrew to the western arm of the mountains. Digging in at the town of Sbeitla, infantry and armor managed to hold off the Germans until February 16. When defenses began to disintegrate during the night, the town was abandoned and troops retreated through the Sbiba and Kasserine passes.

More than one hundred American tanks were destroyed in two days, along with two battalions of artillery overrun, and two battalions of infantry lost. On February 11, 1943, thanks largely to Marshall, Ike finally received his fourth star. On the next day, he heard from Fredendall that his troops were retreating through Kasserine Pass. By February 21, the Germans had pushed through both passes and were poised to seize road junctions leading to the British rear. Allied reinforcements rushed forward. The First Armored Division turned back German probes toward Tébessa, but British armor met a more powerful thrust toward Thala, where four battalions of field artillery from the U.S. Ninth Infantry Division arrived just in time to bolster the sagging defenses. From all along the front and from the rear, every gun and tank that could be brought to bear upon the enemy was being rushed to the critical area. The whole weight of Allied air power in North Africa, including B–17s, was rushed in to support the hard-pressed troops. At nightfall, no one knew what would happen next. On the night of February 22, the Germans began a pullback.

That day, Eisenhower had arrived at the advance command post at Constantine. In discussions with Anderson in the afternoon and by phone with Fredendall, likely German intentions were debated. Eisenhower thought the Germans had lost their momentum and that Fredendall should counterattack at once. Fredendall believed he should wait at least one more day. Eisenhower was right. The battle of the Kasserine Pass was over. In the first test of American fighting ability against the Germans, the U.S. had lost 2,546 men, 103 tanks, 280 vehicles, 18 field guns, 3 anti-tank guns, and an entire antiaircraft battery. On the morning of February 23, the U.S. lines were still holding and the situation was looking better. That afternoon at Tébessa, Eisenhower, Fredendall, General Terry Allen of the First Division, other officers and Truscott met for a conference. Along the front, conditions had vastly improved and there was a tone of optimism.

In conferences with Eisenhower and members of the staff on March 4, Truscott was asked to assess General Fredendall. He replied that he felt the general had lost the confidence of his subordinates and that II Corps could never fight well under his command. He also asserted his belief that Fredendall both disliked and distrusted the British and would never get along well under British command. He advised Ike to relieve Fredendall from II Corps command.

Fredendall had been one of the generals Marshall himself had recommended for major command. This was one of few lapses in his genius for judging leadership candidates. Not only was Fredendall unwilling to cooperate with the British—thereby unwilling to commit to the model of unified command—but he was a weak commander and a physical coward, who kept his engineers busy excavating an elaborate subterranean bunker beneath his headquarters. Marshall later confessed to his official biographer that he "didn't know Fredendall very well," though, curiously, what most "infuriated" him about the discredited II Corps commander was the revelation that "he was foul mouthed." Perhaps Marshall took this trait as an indication that he was "[n]o man for an Allied job."[8]

Marshall had championed Eisenhower, and now, in the wake of the Kasserine debacle, he let his man know what was riding on the performance of the army in North Africa from now on. When Ike's aide-de-camp, U.S. Navy commander Harry Butcher, called on Marshall in Washington, the chief of staff warned him that "Ike's rise or fall depended on the outcome of the Tunisian battle." What Marshall said next made clear that, Ike's "rise or fall" was dependent on the concept of unified command, which Marshall, in turn, was depending on to win the war. "If Rommel & Co. are tossed into the sea, all quibbling, political or otherwise, will be lost in the shouting of the major victory."[9] This warning prompted Eisenhower to turn over II Corps command to George S. Patton Jr. If anyone could rehabilitate this demoralized outfit, Patton could. Marshall concurred.

Omar Bradley was assigned as Patton's deputy. In a letter to Marshall of on May 5, 1943, Eisenhower was able to report "good work and great improvement" under Patton, who was then moved up to command a force that would become the Seventh U.S. Army in the upcoming invasion of Sicily. Bradley was given command of II Corps, and, in the same letter to Marshall, Ike noted that Bradley was "bringing the whole force along in fine style," and that II Corps "must soon be classed as an outstanding tactical organization."[10]

Two days after the letter was written, II Corps captured the seaport of Bizerte and the British took Tunis. On May 13, all German and Italian forces, including Rommel's vaunted Afrika Korps, surrendered. "Unity of Allied effort," Marshall asserted, "had been demonstrated to the world in a most convincing manner, as evidence of the growing concentration of power which will sweep the enemy out of control of the European continent."[11]

CHAPTER 10

Victory Is Certain

ON THE TINY ISLAND OF CORREGIDOR IN MANILA BAY ON MAY 5, 1942, General Jonathan M. Wainwright, MacArthur's successor as U.S. commander in the Philippines, reported, "As I write this we are subjected to terrific air and artillery bombardment and it is unreasonable to expect that we can hold out for long. We have done our best . . . and although beaten we are still unashamed." Five months to the day after Pearl Harbor, Wainwright surrendered. The effects of the desperate resistance of the small Philippines force, Marshall noted, "holding as they did a sizeable portion of Japanese strength," bought time for men and materials to be shipped to Australia as the base for operations in the Southwest Pacific. With the U.S. Navy's victories in the Coral Sea and at Midway Island, the Japanese offensive "had definitely been checked." As American forces held island bases from Hawaii to Australia, Marshall's Pacific commanders were free to prepare operations to drive the Japanese back.[1]

On August 7, 1942, while Eisenhower was planning Operation Torch, the First Marine Division began the first U.S. ground offensive of the war by assaulting Guadalcanal in the Solomon Islands. Having moved into the region in March 1942, the Japanese were intent on taking Guadalcanal in order to build an airfield and solidify a base on the island as part of their plan to conquer Australia and New Zealand and gain dominance of the South Pacific. To stop the Japanese advance, the U.S. Joint Chiefs of Staff deployed the Marines and on August 1, the First Battalion, quickly followed by the Third Battalion, landed in complete surprise and established a beachhead without opposition. Their objective was to seize the nearly complete airfield and an anchorage at Tulagi in the Solomon Islands. Although the airstrip was regularly bombed and shelled, American planes were still able to fly, ensuring that Japanese efforts to build and maintain ground forces were prohibitively costly. Throughout the hard fighting in dense jungles, the outcome of the campaign would remain in doubt for four months.

Sailing from Hawaii in three convoys beginning on November 25, the Twenty-fifth Division was well under way on November 30 when an order was received from the Joint Chiefs of Staff to proceed not to Australia and MacArthur's command, but rather to Noumea, New Caledonia, 800 miles to the north, to prepare to relieve the First Marine Division on Guadalcanal. Reinforced in the autumn by two regiments of the recently formed U.S. Army Americal Division, the Twenty-fifth Division was under command of Major General Alexander M. "Sandy" Patch Jr. and his deputy, Major General J. Lawton Collins.

Collins was one of the promising officers whose name Marshall had jotted in his little black book. He had served under Marshall as an instructor at the Infantry School, Fort Benning. Collins was subsequently executive officer of the Twenty-third Brigade, Manila, and assistant chief of staff for intelligence in the Philippine Division (1933–1934). Promoted to lieutenant colonel in June of 1940, he was appointed chief of staff, VII Corps, in the temporary rank of colonel in January 1941. Following the attack on Pearl Harbor, Collins was designated chief of staff to General Delos C. Emmons and traveled with him to Hawaii to assist in reorganizing the islands' defenses. Named commanding general of the Twenty-fifth Infantry Division in May 1942, he had expected the division to stay in Hawaii to defend against a possible Japanese invasion, but was instead ordered by the South Pacific Area commander, Admiral William F. "Bull" Halsey, to "eliminate all Japanese forces" on Guadalcanal. Opting to "avoid all frontal attacks" Collins decided instead to go after open ridges by flanking maneuvers, then trap the enemy in valleys "where they could be forced to surrender or be destroyed by artillery and mortar fire."[2]

While Collins led the Twenty-fifth "Tropical Lightning" Division in jungle fighting, George Marshall, from his Pentagon office, was in command of the largest army in American history, with more than five million soldiers and more than a thousand generals. Supply routes stretched 59,000 miles. No general in the history of warfare had ever been required to orchestrate such a global conflict. He tracked the fighting on Guadalcanal, even as a debate opened in Washington, D.C., between the victors of the North African campaign over where to go next. It was that kind of war. Close-quarters jungle combat in the Pacific raging simultaneously with a far-ranging fight over miles of desert literally half a world away. Marshall's job was to manage both theaters, radically different as they were and both clamoring for men and supplies.

Having crossed the Atlantic on the *Queen Mary*, the luxury liner now in battle dress as a troop transport, Winston Churchill arrived in Washington for a conference he had requested. It was code-named Trident, and he hoped to use it to win final American approval to follow a conquest of Sicily—Operation Husky—with an invasion of mainland Italy and additional actions in the eastern Mediterranean as well as a drive into the Balkans.

With the needs of two widely separated, radically different theaters already jostling for their share of attention in his mind, Marshall, who had only reluctantly acceded to the North African and Sicilian campaigns, argued passionately that Churchill's plan to lavish forces on mainland Italy and then elsewhere in Europe's "soft underbelly" would impose an unacceptable further delay on the assembly of sufficient forces in the United Kingdom to execute a successful cross-Channel operation. The original intention had been to mount the invasion in 1942. The North African episode had pushed that to 1943, and now Churchill's plans would postpone what Marshall conceived of as the main event of the war in the European theater to late 1944. Moreover, the drain on resources would be such that the final pushes in the Pacific would also be delayed, and the war in that theater also prolonged. With the tense and at times acrimonious talks close to breaking down, Secretary of War Henry Stimson noted, "It is taking all Marshall's tact and adroitness to steer the conference through to a result which will not be a surrender [to Churchill and the British] but which will not be an open clash [with them]."[3] If unified command was difficult to carry out in the field, it was proving, if anything, even harder at the very highest levels. Still, Marshall dared not give up on the concept, the effectiveness of which, he believed, had been amply proved by the success of the North African campaign.

Weary and frustrated conferees finally settled on a compromise that left both sides with half a loaf. The British got their desire to follow Operation Husky with an invasion of mainland Italy; the Americans won a British pledge of the cross-Channel invasion of France—now named Operation Overlord—on May 1, 1944, subject to Eisenhower's approval in a conference with Churchill in Algiers. Like Marshall, Churchill was keenly aware of the fragility of unified command, and he suddenly protested that he did not want to be put in a position where he could be accused of "exerting his wiles" on Ike. He therefore proposed that Marshall scrap a plan to travel to the Pacific to confer with MacArthur and Halsey and instead accompany him to Algiers. Concerned that the Pacific theater was being neglected at the top levels—which meant neglected by him—Marshall was not happy with Churchill's suggestion. Nevertheless, in the interest of promoting and preserving unity of command, he swallowed his feelings and agreed. Stimson confined his own concern to a page in his diary: "To think of picking out the strongest man there is in America, and Marshall sure is that today, and send him off on a difficult and rather dangerous trip across the Atlantic Ocean where he is not needed except for Churchill's purposes is I think going pretty far."[4]

They took off on May 26 and, after an overnight stopover at Gibraltar, boarded Churchill's new plane, a converted Lancaster bomber, for the final leg of the journey, arriving, with fighter escorts, in Algiers on May 28. As it turned out, Marshall need not have feared that he was squandering his time on this errand; for, en route, Churchill changed his view of Marshall from "rugged soldier and a magnificent organizer and builder of armies" to that of "a statesman with a penetrating and commanding view of the whole scene."[5] Marshall, it seems, was persuading Churchill to see the United States as an equal in every aspect of the war.

Once they were in Algiers, Churchill carried on at times like a British barrister arguing a case in London's Old Bailey, with Eisenhower a jury of one and, at other times, like a member of Parliament presenting a bill for a vote. He was, Eisenhower later wrote, "at his eloquent best in painting a rosy picture" of opportunities that he foresaw opening up with the capture of Sicily. He insisted that he had no intention of interfering with preparations for Overlord in 1944, but he was concerned to persuade both Ike and Marshall of the necessity of the Allies' rapidly exploiting "any opportunities arising out of the fall of Sicily" for "the quick capture of southern Italy."[6] Both Americans were wary; they believed Churchill had doubts about the successful outcome of a European invasion, and this sounded exactly like a justification for putting off Overlord even further.

On June 3, General Montgomery arrived at the conference to present his plan for taking Sicily. A man the Americans found easy to dislike because of his egotistically prickly manner, lack of tact, and absence of any appreciation for the feelings or intelligence of others, he had once ordered a chain-smoking Ike—his *superior* officer—to put out his cigarette. (Montgomery, an abstemious nonsmoker, forbade cigarettes in his headquarters.)

Marshall, who made it a point of professionalism to tolerate virtually everyone, disliked Monty immediately. Dismissing all ideas for Husky proposed by senior U.S. officers, including a daringly brilliant one Patton had proposed, as "woolly thinking" about the use of infantry, Montgomery presented a plan that gave the lead role in Husky solely to his own British Eighth Army, relegating Patton's Seventh U.S. Army to providing flanking support. When he learned that Montgomery's plan was being adopted, Patton confided to his diary, "The U.S. is getting gypped. This is what you get when the Commander-in-Chief [Eisenhower] ceases to be an American and becomes an ally."[7] Marshall was equally disappointed, but he believed that Operation Husky had been undertaken largely at British insistence, so he was reluctant to push an American plan onto it. Besides, Eisenhower, the supreme Allied commander, was more than willing to give Monty the ball, and Marshall did not want to compromise unity of command by openly disagreeing with his own commander. Musical genius, it has been said, has as much to do with silences as with sounded notes; Marshall proved that military genius, at the executive level of management demanded by a vast multinational alliance, had as much to do with self-restraint as with self-expression.

Believing that any sacrifice he had made on behalf of the U.S. Army and its role in Husky had been in the service of maintaining unified command, Marshall returned to Washington on a U.S. Army Air Forces C–54 transport, with two enlisted men and a second lieutenant who had been wounded in Tunisia on board. On his arrival at the Pentagon, he was upset to learn that he had been invited by the commandant of the officer training school at the Armored Forces Center, Fort Knox, Kentucky, to attend the graduation of his stepson, Allen Brown. Marshall replied by letter that he would not attend and that he had hoped Allen could get through school without his identity as stepson of the chief of staff even being disclosed. He then wrote separately to Allen that if he would care to get an immediate assignment to an armored division in Africa, "I could possibly arrange that." A farewell party for Allen a few weeks later at the house in Leesburg brought the whole Marshall family together for the last time during the war.

The night before Allen was to leave for Africa, during a debate among the young men about which army branch was most important—tanks, anti-aircraft, or artillery—Marshall piped in with mock humility, "Of course I am only a lowly foot soldier. I do not belong in such august company as that of the Artillery, Anti-aircraft, and Tanks, but I would say—when the fighting is the fiercest, it is invariably the Infantry that carries the ball over for the touchdown."[8]

On July 10, 1943, with Second Lieutenant Allen Brown now in North Africa as a replacement officer in the First Armored Division, his stepfather was ensconced in an office in the outer ring of the Pentagon, waiting for confirmation from Eisenhower's headquarters in the St. George's Hotel in Algiers that Operation Husky had begun. Reminding him that the invasion of Sicily was but one part of the chief of staff's global war were maps and reports marking the scope of American commitments on land, at sea, and in the air on every continent.

By July 1, 1943, more than a thousand Eighth U.S. Air Force heavy bombers based in Great Britain were flying missions against Germany, which forced Hitler to increase production of fighter aircraft at the expense of bombers and to withdraw experienced single-engine fighter pilots from the Russian and Mediterranean fronts for the defense of Germany. Japan's prolonged conquest of the Philippines and the defeats suffered by its navy had upset its timetable for operations in the Southwest Pacific, allowing U.S. forces to seize the offensive. Convoys from the United States had delivered to Russia more than 3,000 airplanes, 2,400 tanks, 16,000 Jeeps, 80,000 trucks, 7,000 motorcycles, 130,000 field telephones, and 75,000 tons of explosives. More than 10,000 Army Engineer troops were building a 1,400-mile Alaska Military Highway. Driving the Japanese out of Alaska's Aleutian Islands had cost the lives of 512 American soldiers and 2,550 Japanese. U.S. troops were deployed throughout the Caribbean and in nine countries in South America. Pursuant to President Roosevelt's signing a law that created the Women's Army Auxiliary Corps (WAAC) on May 14, 1942, more than 65,000 women were serving in some 240 posts in the United States and abroad. In training camps from coast to coast, hundreds of thousands of inductees were learning military basics and being versed in all the technical skills required by the mechanized, highly mobile military Marshall had advocated, which was now operating in climates ranging from the subarctic to the tropics and in all kinds of terrain.

To conquer the inverted triangle that is the island of Sicily, dominated by the majestic Mount Etna volcano, Montgomery's plan called for his Eighth Army to land on the southeast coast in the vicinity of the ancient city of Syracuse. Patton's Seventh Army and Bradley's II Corps would come ashore to the south and west at Gela and advance north to protect Montgomery's left flank. Montgomery's objective was Messina, a large port separated from the Italian mainland by a three-mile-wide strait. Its swift capture would bottle up the Axis forces on Sicily, preventing their withdrawal to fight another day. Eisenhower had estimated that the capture of Messina could be achieved in two weeks, but he and his mentor in Washington found that stronger German resistance than anticipated, combined with competition between Patton and Montgomery, made Sicily one of the bloodier episodes in American military history.

The mission of General Patton's Seventh Army was to assault the southeast portion of Sicily in conjunction with the British Eighth Army under Montgomery and capture it as a base for later operations. The Americans were to take airfields close to the small ports of Gela and Licata and prepare for operations by the British. Seventh Army was to conduct simultaneous assaults under cover of darkness on D-Day at Sampieri, Gela, and Licata, capture and secure the airfields and the port of Licata by D plus two, then extend the beachhead, establish contact with the British Eighth Army, and move to high ground to prevent a German counterattack out of the northwest.

Assaults called CENT-DIME under General Bradley's II Corps were to capture and secure an airfield at Ponte Olivo by daylight of D plus one, another near Comiso by daylight on D plus two, a third near Biscari by dark and then make contact with Truscott's Third Infantry Division on the left. The Third's operation called for capturing the port and airfield at Licata by dark of D-Day, extending the beachhead, and making contact with II Corps. Because there were no suitable major ports to handle oceangoing shipping, the invasion forces were to be supplied and maintained over the assault beaches and through the smaller ports for a period of at least thirty days.

With the exception of a slight delay in the hour of landing occasioned by the bad weather, the assault went almost exactly as planned. Battalions had landed before they were discovered and quickly cleared the beaches of all resistance. In little more than an hour, ten infantry battalions had landed, including the Rangers with supporting tanks. In seven hours, they seized the first day's objectives and were pushing reconnaissance far out to the front. Airfield, town, and port were in American hands, the beaches and the port were organized, and additional troops and supplies were flowing ashore. Resistance had been smothered by the speed and violence of the assault and more than a thousand prisoners taken. U.S. casualties were a little more than a hundred. By nightfall on July 10, contact had been established among all elements along a fifty-mile front, and every unit was pressing reconnaissance to make and maintain contact with the withdrawing enemy force.

During a visit to Third Infantry Division command post at noon on July 14, Patton reported that on the east coast of Sicily, Montgomery's Eighth Army had taken Augusta and was advancing against only moderate enemy resistance. A report from Patton to Marshall on July 18 read, "Thus far things have gone better than we had a right to expect." Pleased with the events, and proud of the men he had chosen as commanders, Marshall prodded the War Department press relations officers to highlight them by pointing out that Forty-fifth Division commander Major General Troy Middleton had been a decorated hero in World War I, and that General Lucian Truscott of the Third Division was one of the first U.S. officers to go to Britain in 1942. Further, Truscott had gone along with British and Canadian Commandos in a raid on the French port of Dieppe in the summer of 1942.[9]

General Marshall's P.R. men had no need to trumpet Patton, who was his own publicity machine. Wearing an enameled helmet, cavalry boots, and an ivory-handled revolver, he was a bold contrast to Bradley of II Corps, whom war correspondent Ernie Pyle had dubbed the "GI general," and the Third Division's equally earthy Lucian Truscott. Still bristling over the rejection of his proposed plan for Sicily, which had the Seventh U.S. Army landing on the north coast to capture Palermo, Patton gloated when Montgomery became bogged down by German resistance. Because this resistance wrecked Monty's original timetable, leaving Seventh Army with nothing to do, Patton decided to shift the army to the north and, on his own initiative, take Palermo. Patton told Truscott that Third Division would need to take Porto Empedocle, but that he had orders not to do so because a battle might risk exposure of Montgomery's flank. Truscott responded confidently that he could take the objective without too much trouble; all Patton had to do was give the word. When Patton repeated that he had orders not to attack Empedocle, Truscott took the hint and declared that high command could surely have no objection to his making a "reconnaissance in force" toward Agrigento on his own responsibility. Of this conspiratorial conversation between the generals Truscott later wrote, "Patton, with something of the air of the cat that had swallowed the canary, agreed that he thought they would not."[10]

When Patton left, Truscott set the wheels in motion. In his plan, a reconnaissance in force would move to Agrigento to "clear up an uncertain situation." On July 14, the Ranger battalion would circle around Agrigento during the night and seize the port. If all went well, Truscott could report to Patton by noon the next day that Agrigento was his. Following the progress of the mission from a forward command post, Truscott learned at midafternoon that the attackers had isolated the port. After some street fighting, Italian defenders gave up. To Truscott's surprise and amazement the improvised and officially illicit maneuver ended with heavy enemy casualties, 6,000 Italian army prisoners, and the capture of hundreds of their tanks, vehicles, and artillery pieces.

Of this bold maneuver Patton later said that had it failed he would have been relieved of command. When British general Harold Alexander learned of the capture of Porto Empedocle on July 18, he issued Field Orders No. 1, giving Patton permission to form a provisional corps, including the Third Division, to head west to take Palermo. Describing capture of the port as Patton's lodestar, and observing that Patton hated playing second fiddle to Montgomery in Sicily or anywhere else, Truscott depicted the champion of tank warfare's looking ahead to a spectacular sweep into Palermo as the first great exploit for American armor. As for Marshall, he knew enough to refrain from complaining about success. As the war continued, Eisenhower would have ample occasion to complain to Marshall about Patton as a loose cannon or, as he sometimes called him, a "problem child." Marshall would listen, but would never order Ike to do one thing or another concerning Patton. His directive was always the same. If Patton, difficult as he was, continued to prove more an asset than a liability, then he (Marshall) was prepared to take the heat from the British and, on more than one occasion, the American public. If, on the other hand, Eisenhower ever felt that Patton proved more trouble than he was worth, it was up to Ike to relieve him.

The drive for Palermo began. After three days of house-to-house fighting, the city fell, and 53,000 Italian soldiers were captured. With this stunning victory, the Allies suddenly controlled half of Sicily. But capturing Sicily's biggest city was not enough for Patton. He wanted to humiliate Montgomery at least as badly as he wanted to defeat the Germans, and he now set his sights on beating Monty to Messina.

On August 3, while planning the drive on Messina, Patton visited the Fifteenth Evacuation Hospital near Nicosia. Among the sick and wounded, he encountered Private Charles H. Kuhl, Company L, Twenty-sixth Infantry Regiment (First Division). Kuhl did not appear to be wounded. When Patton asked him what was the matter, Kuhl replied "I guess I can't take it," whereupon Patton cursed him, slapped him across the face with his gloves, then grabbed him by the scruff of his neck and kicked him out of the hospital tent. The incident went largely unremarked except by those who witnessed it, but on August 10, Patton toured the Ninety-third Evacuation Hospital, where he came across Private Paul G. Bennett, C Battery, Seventeenth Field Artillery, II Corps. Like Kuhl, he appeared uninjured. Patton asked him what his problem was, and Bennett replied that it was his "nerves." Again, Patton exploded, slapped Bennett's helmet liner off his head, and bellowed at him, "You're going back to the front lines and you may get shot and killed, but you're going to fight. If you don't, I'll stand you up against a wall and have a firing squad kill you on purpose." Reaching for his pistol, Patton threatened to shoot him right then and there.[11]

In time—and soon—these two brutal incidents, savoring of Nazi tyranny, would create a major public relations crisis for Marshall as the senior officer in an army dedicated to the defense of democracy and justice. For now, however, the greater problem was posed by the Twenty-ninth Panzer Grenadier Division, which stood in the way of Third Division's conquest of Messina. After a series of unsuccessful attacks, Truscott's Second Battalion, Thirtieth Infantry, reinforced with batteries of artillery and a platoon of tanks, was able to land at Sant'Agata on August 8, cutting off escape by some of the Germans. However, the bulk of the German force had withdrawn the previous night.

Nevertheless, on August 16, the Seventh Infantry overcame the last German resistance and by nightfall was on the heights overlooking Messina. After one hundred rounds of artillery were lobbed onto the mainland of Europe at the Germans escaping into Italy, Rangers entered the city. On the heights above, Truscott accepted the surrender of Messina by civil functionaries. When the senior Italian military official presented his Beretta pistol to Truscott as a gesture of capitulation, Truscott told him to go back into the city and wait to make the formal surrender to General Patton. Directed by Keyes to delay entering Messina until Patton arrived, Truscott arranged for transportation with motorcycles and scout car escorts. When Patton appeared the next day with characteristic flurry, he barked, "What in the hell are you all standing around for?" Truscott replied, "We were waiting for you, General." Thanks to Lucian Truscott, Patton had beaten Montgomery to Messina.[12]

⊢═══⊣

While Patton's Seventh Army was (without authorization) racing Montgomery to Messina, Marshall withheld his judgment and held his tongue. He was in Quebec, Canada, at a meeting between President Roosevelt and Winston Churchill to talk about Italy and settle the question of Operation Overlord. It was agreed that the supreme commander of the culminating invasion of Europe would be George Marshall, with Eisenhower succeeding him in

Washington as U.S. Army chief of staff. He looked forward to this new assignment—the biggest in the war—as he returned to the Pentagon to issue his second biennial report. Covering the period of July 1, 1941, to June 30, 1943, the report was 30,000 words in length and concluded, "The end [of the war] is not clearly in sight but victory is certain."[13]

CHAPTER 11

Mighty Endeavor

On August 24, 1943, Eisenhower gave George C. Marshall a performance assessment of their mutual longtime friend and comrade in arms George S. Patton Jr. Eisenhower's letter began with a glowing account of the operations of Patton's Seventh Army in Sicily, predicting that "[they] are going to be classed as a model of swift conquest" for the "prodigious marches, the incessant attacks, the refusal to be halted." But Ike continued: "George Patton continues to exhibit some of those unfortunate personal traits of which you and I have always known and which during this campaign caused me some most uncomfortable days."

Marshall knew what Ike was referring to. Eisenhower had managed to secure the cooperation of war correspondents in Sicily to keep the lid on the two slapping incidents, though he had not let them go unnoticed. Ike sent Patton a stinging personal (though off-the-record) reprimand, and Patton apologized not only to the two soldiers, but to much of the Seventh Army, unit by unit. Eisenhower told Marshall, "Personally, I believe that he is cured—not only because of his great personal loyalty to you and to me but because he is so avid for recognition as a great military commander that he will ruthlessly suppress any habit of his own that will tend to jeopardize it. Aside from this one thing, he has qualities that we cannot afford to lose unless he ruins himself."[1]

But neither Patton, nor Eisenhower, nor Marshall would get off so easily. Despite the voluntary news blackout, accounts of the slapping incidents made their way through Sicily by way of the army grapevine and, with "lightning speed," crossed the Atlantic via what Ike termed "the gossip route," where they were picked up and broadcast nationally in November by muckraking Washington columnist and radio commentator Drew Pearson. The public outrage was instant and, at first, apparently overwhelming. Eisenhower asked Marshall if he wanted Patton removed. Marshall was all about professional self-control and military decorum. In terms of personality and conduct, Patton could not have been more different from Marshall nor more offensive to his ideal of proper martial bearing, which had been founded on the likes of John Pershing. But precisely because Marshall was a professional, who focused on results more than process, he replied to Ike with his usual response: as long as Patton was an asset, retain him; if he proved a liability, remove him. Like the great manager that he was, Marshall turned the focus on performance and away from personality.

Meanwhile, with the Sicilian campaign completed, Patton had presided over the dissolution of Seventh Army as part of a restructuring in which a newly formed Fifth Army, commanded by Mark W. Clark, would invade the Italian mainland via an amphibious landing at Salerno. Patton assumed that he would be put at the head of the ground forces in Operation Overlord, as did the German high command. Eisenhower went against the tide of expectation by recommending to Marshall, "To my mind, Bradley should be the United States Assaulting Army Commander."[2] Marshall did not object. Both he and Eisenhower had great confidence in Omar Bradley, and both believed that he would be more capable of sustaining a cooperative relationship with the British than Patton would. Moreover, both Marshall and Eisenhower assessed Patton as a tactician more than a strategist. With his tactical combat experience, he would be better used leading an army in the field than coordinating the entire invasion from the rear. Patton was profoundly disappointed. Even worse, Ike kept him out of the action for the eleventh months leading up to the Normandy landings. He had decided on the bold—and, to generations of military historians, controversial—stratagem of using Patton as a decoy, exploiting the Germans' belief that, as the Allies' best field commander, Patton would lead the invasion and would do so across the Pas-de-Calais, not down the coast at Normandy. There is no record of Marshall's participation in this decision, other than his approval of Bradley as ground force commander. As for Patton, he always believed that he had lost the Overlord command because of the slapping incidents.

In the meantime, Marshall looked forward to *his* role in Overlord, which, he expected, would be as supreme Allied commander. On September 1, 1943, his four-year term as chief of staff would expire. Except for Douglas MacArthur's twenty years earlier, no chief of staff's tenure had ever been extended, so Marshall believed he was about to swap positions with Eisenhower, as contemplated at the Quebec Conference. President Roosevelt put this exchange off, however, by announcing that Marshall would remain chief of staff indefinitely because of his service to the nation.

Still chief of staff, Marshall accompanied Roosevelt to the president's conference in Cairo with Churchill and Generalissimo Chiang Kai-shek of China to address the long-neglected China-Burma-India (C-B-I) theater of war. The two-part Cairo conference, code-named Sextant (November 23–26; December 3–7, 1943), sandwiched a "Big Three" meeting in Teheran, Iran (code-named Eureka, November 28-December 1), at which Roosevelt and Marshall met Soviet Premier Joseph Stalin for the first time. (Stalin did not attend Sextant because the USSR was not at war with Japan.) While Roosevelt and the man he called "Uncle Joe" talked about Overlord as Stalin's long-awaited second front, Churchill continued to press for his Italian and Balkans strategy, in part to prevent the Red Army from cementing Eastern Europe into a postwar Soviet sphere of influence. At one point, Stalin bluntly challenged Churchill's commitment to Overlord. Chomping his Cuban cigar, Churchill replied that if requirements for the invasion of France in May 1944 were met, it would the "the duty of the British government to hurl every scrap of strength across the Channel."[3] Marshall was as relieved to hear this as Stalin.

The Teheran Conference ended with a secret Big Three "manifesto" setting out three goals: invading Normandy in May 1944 (Operation Overlord), launching a simultaneous invasion of southern France (Operation

Anvil), and pressing the campaign in Italy that had commenced on September 9, 1943. The last goal worried Marshall, who believed that the Italian campaign would drain resources from Overlord and Anvil. After successful landings at Salerno by the Fifth Army under General Mark Clark, with the objective of taking the port of Naples, the invasion plan called for Fifth Army to link up with the British invading farther east to form a continuous front across Italy. Instead, both the Americans and the British ran into fierce German resistance that stalled the northward advance as winter closed in. Always the realist, Marshall believed that the Italian campaign would take much longer and require much greater resources than Churchill or anyone else had imagined. He was determined to stand his ground and retain for Overlord and Anvil as much of the Allied resources as possible.

While Stalin made his way back from Teheran to Moscow to resume direct command of the Red Army as it drove the German invaders back toward their fatherland, Roosevelt and Churchill returned to Cairo for the second part of the conference. Still pending was a public announcement of the choice of Marshall to swap positions with Eisenhower and take command of Operation Overlord.

Roosevelt had put off the announcement in the hope that Marshall would ask for the appointment, but, despite the decision at Quebec, Marshall had not raised the issue. At a meeting with Harry Hopkins on December 4, 1943, Marshall had told FDR's confidant that he would go along with whatever decision the president made. Consequently, Roosevelt invited Marshall to lunch in Cairo, hoping that he would push the issue and forthrightly ask for the job. After what Marshall called "a great deal of beating about the bush," the president finally asked Marshall what he wanted to do. Marshall replied that he would "cheerfully go whatever way" Roosevelt wished.

Suddenly, it became clear to FDR why he had found it difficult to pull the trigger on the decision. The president seemed to ruminate for a moment before he declared that he didn't feel he could sleep at ease "if you were out of the country." After a long silence, he added, "Then it will be Eisenhower."[4]

If Marshall felt any pangs of disappointment, he made no protest. While it was true that, as chief of staff, Marshall was at the pinnacle of the army command structure, he was keenly aware that leading the invasion of Europe was the biggest job of the war. At least he would have the consolation of public acclaim. *Time* magazine would soon proclaim Marshall its "Man of the Year" for

1943, stating that "American democracy is the stuff Marshall is made of." But, more important, the fact was that President Roosevelt had grown to rely on Marshall precisely because he was equally as adept and authoritative working with political and national leaders as he was with military commanders. Realizing this, Marshall had decided to leave the decision to the president.

More than Eisenhower, Marshall was the prototype of the new kind of American military executive. The complex Allied endeavor of World War II called for a top soldier who could straddle the realms of diplomacy and military science. The need for such a hybrid would only increase in the postwar world—and is taken for granted today. Battlefield training and experience are no longer sufficient for high command, which has become a job of global geopolitical scope. The trend toward this versatility began in World War II, and Marshall led the way.

The public announcement of Eisenhower's appointment was made shortly after Marshall and the president ended their lunch. Instead of returning directly to Washington from Cairo, Marshall headed east by way of Ceylon to Australia to meet with Douglas MacArthur, only to learn that MacArthur was at the front in New Guinea. MacArthur's absence might well have been interpreted as a deliberate snub, had Marshall chosen to see it this way. Instead, he set out for New Guinea.

It was their first meeting since 1935, when Marshall was a colonel training the Illinois National Guard in Chicago and MacArthur retired as chief of staff. Now chief of staff himself, Marshall was concerned that the notoriously egotistical MacArthur was feeling neglected and was bickering with Admiral Ernest J. King, the chief of naval operations (CNO) and commander in chief of the U.S. Fleet. Marshall wanted to put a stop to interservice squabbling, especially at the highest level. Moreover, he was eager to personally brief MacArthur on the Cairo and Teheran conferences and to tell him that China no longer figured centrally in the Allies' Pacific strategy. It had been decided to make the assault on the Japanese home islands from the west.

So Marshall met with MacArthur in New Guinea—a gesture that impressed the prima donna—and, while he did what he could to repair relations between the army and navy's top commanders, he carefully laid out the overall strategy in the Pacific. This mission accomplished, Marshall continued the voyage home, arriving three days before Christmas.

Now Marshall engaged in a heavy round of conferences and official functions. He summoned Major General J. Lawton "Lightning Joe" Collins from the South Pacific to Washington and, on January 2, 1944, settled back in his chair to listen to all that the commander of the Twenty-fifth Division had to say about the momentous, hard-won victory at Guadalcanal in the Solomon Islands (August 1942 to February 1943). When Collins completed his narrative of the final stages of Guadalcanal, he ventured to tell Marshall that he hoped he could move up a rung from division to corps command. Marshall replied that he had raised that very question with MacArthur. With what Collins described as a rare twinkle in his eyes, Marshall added that MacArthur had said that forty-eight-year-old Collins was "too young." (MacArthur was sixteen years Collins's senior.)

Marshall closed the meeting by informing Collins that his presence was desired at a reception for Eisenhower the next day at Washington's exclusive Alibi Club. The guest list was stellar. From the administration were Secretary of War Henry Louis Stimson, Undersecretary Robert R. Patterson, Assistant Secretary John J. McCloy, and Director of War Mobilization James F. Byrnes. On behalf of the Congress were representatives Andrew J. May, Walter G. Andrews, R. Ewing Thomason, and senators Warren Austin and Wallace H. White. Financier Bernard Baruch, the powerful confidant of Woodrow Wilson and FDR—and a friend of Marshall's—was also there. Former chief of naval operations Admiral Harold R. Stark addressed the gathering with a report on the status of the war against Nazi U-boats in the North Atlantic. Army Air Forces chief Hap Arnold talked about the air war against Germany and was followed by Lieutenant General George C. Kenney, who summarized the air campaigns in the South Pacific. At Marshall's request, "Lightning Joe" Collins himself discussed the wrap-up of Guadalcanal and the campaign in New Georgia. Eisenhower reported on Operation Torch, the success of Operation Husky, and the ongoing invasion of Italy. As for Operation Overlord, it was mentioned only vaguely, and at the conclusion of Ike's remarks, Marshall led the guests in lifting their glasses to toast the president and Eisenhower, supreme commander of Overlord.

The next morning, General Collins and his wife, Gladys, left the capital for White Sulphur Springs, West Virginia. A secluded resort where people had been "taking the waters" since 1778, it had a hotel, the Greenbrier, and small guest cottages. Taken over by the army ostensibly as a military hospital, the Greenbrier also served as a place for high-profile visitors on army business to escape the prying eyes of the press. It was an ideal out-of-sight spot for Marshall to sequester visiting generals.

Collins and Gladys had been there only a day or two when they were invited to dinner at the house of the commander of the hospital, Colonel Clyde McK. Beck. Stating it would be a small, informal party, Mrs. Beck stressed that guests be on time. Her reason for insisting on punctuality was revealed when the last guests arrived. Surprised to see General and Mrs. Eisenhower enter, Collins had the impression that Ike was just as taken aback to see *him* there. "Why Joe!" Ike exclaimed. "I didn't know you were down here. I understand you are coming over to join us!"

Startled to learn in this offhand manner that he was evidently to be transferred to Ike's European Theater, Collins correctly assumed that Marshall had dismissed MacArthur's view that he was too young to head a corps and had said so to Eisenhower. The orders assigning him to Eisenhower's command were issued on January 19, 1944.[5]

The episode was both typical of Marshall and out of character. Typical was the chief of staff's genius for putting men where he wanted them—without having to override anyone's objections. Collins was a valuable piece of manpower. Marshall wanted him elevated to corps command, but MacArthur did not. Rather than tangle with the supreme egotist of the Pacific theater, Marshall moved Collins up in Europe. As for the manner in which he did this, the usually direct Marshall chose an almost whimsically roundabout route. We can only assume that this was part of his deft effort to make an end run around MacArthur by presenting Collins's transfer not as a discussion or even an order, but a fait accompli. Such was military diplomacy and military psychology at the very highest level.

On January 22, 1944, 50,000 U.S. troops landed north of Naples at Anzio. They met little opposition, but, despite this, their commander, Major General John P. Lucas, chose to solidify the beachhead rather than quickly push inland. The delay gave the German commander, Field Marshal Albert

Kesselring, time to move infantry divisions, tanks, and artillery into the region. The result was that, instead of an end-run around the German defenses strung across the Italian boot followed by a rapid advance north to Rome that would strand the entire German force in southern Italy, Anzio became a bloodbath that, just as Marshall had feared, diverted ships and landing craft (a type of vessel in short supply throughout the war) from being shifted to England for Overlord.

By May 1944, British and Americans in the mountains were still blocked from advancing, and U.S. troops remained stuck at Anzio. In hopes of breaking out from the beachhead as part of a coordinated move on all fronts, Mark Clark replaced Lucas with Lucian Truscott. The renewed Allied push began on May 11 with the elimination by bombing and a ground assault of a venerated monastery atop Monte Cassino, which had been a German stronghold. To the west, U.S. and Italian troops (now fighting on the side of the Allies) crossed the Rapido River, aiming to link up with Truscott's force at Anzio. On May 23, Truscott's men finally broke out, and after hard fighting drove north to the Alban Hills south of Rome.

A week later, General Clark sent a message to the Pentagon marked "personal" for Marshall. It informed him that his stepson, Second Lieutenant Allen Tupper Brown, had been killed by a sniper as he climbed out of his tank on the road to Rome. Marshall went to his quarters at Fort Myer to break the news to Katherine. He found her standing at a window in her room. "A blessed numbness comes to one at a time like this," she wrote in her memoir. "I could not comprehend George's words." She had only one thought—to tell Allen's wife in New York—and, in a rare exercise of his authority for a personal purpose, Marshall ordered a plane to take him and his wife there.[6]

Two days later, he was back at work. On June 4, 1944, the city of Rome fell, having been abandoned by the Germans. At four o'clock (GMT) on that morning in stormy southeast England, Dwight Eisenhower had met with all of the commanders for the invasion of France, scheduled for the next day, June 5. They heard a dour but canny Scot, Group Captain James Martin Stagg, chief of the Meteorological Committee, present the latest dismal weather forecast for the English Channel and the invasion beaches on the Normandy coast. Drenched by nearly a week of heavy, incessant rain, the southern half of England was one vast military camp. Cut off from the other half of the island, it was piled high with supplies and equipment and crammed with impatient soldiers who had been given their invasion orders. "A mighty host," in the words of Supreme Commander Eisenhower, they waited for him to issue the signal for them to vault the English Channel in the greatest amphibious assault ever attempted.[7]

But he could not. In view of the weather, he ordered a one-day postponement. On June 5, Stagg and his team of forecasters predicted that for about thirty-six hours on June 6 the rough weather conditions in Normandy would subside enough for the landings to proceed. Eisenhower said he didn't like it, but to postpone again presented the even worse prospect of forfeiting both favorable lunar and tidal conditions as well as the element of surprise. Accordingly, he gave the order.

His coded cable to Marshall read: "Halcyon plus 5 finally and definitely confirmed."[8] It meant that the operation that was to have kicked off on June 1, was now set for dawn on June 6, with paratroop landings behind the enemy lines commencing five hours earlier (7:30 P.M., June 5, Washington, D.C., time).

From all ports capable of handling troop transports and warships of every kind and size, an invasion armada of 4,000 vessels, divided into task forces, sailed at staggered times to a rendezvous point, then crossed the Channel, arriving off the Normandy beaches just before dawn. Following intense naval and aerial bombardment, landing craft were to head ashore at 6:30 A.M.

As planes carrying the Eighty-second and 101st airborne divisions took off in England, Marshall was in his dress uniform, attending a reception at the embassy of the Soviet Union, where Ambassador Andrei Gromyko awarded him Russia's highest military decoration for a foreigner. The ceremony and medal were real, but his well-publicized attendance was a ruse designed to give the impression to all the world—especially to the German high command, which anticipated an invasion any day led by Patton at the Pas-de-Calais—of business as usual. Nevertheless, as soon as courtesy permitted, Marshall left the embassy and returned to Fort Myer, only to decide that, because there was nothing he could do about Overlord at this point, it was "much better to get a good night's sleep and be ready for whatever the morning might bring."

A few hours later, an excited War Department duty officer pounded on the door of Quarters No. 1, waking Katherine Marshall. When she refused to disturb her husband, the officer handed her a decoded cable and waited.

"And what would you have General Marshall do about it?" she asked.[9]

It was a confirmation of the D-Day invasion.

Marshall reported for work at his usual hour and spent much of the day answering letters and notes of consolation on his stepson's death. Whatever he might have been thinking about D-Day went unrecorded.

That night, President Roosevelt broadcast a radio address to the nation in the form of a prayer:

> Almighty God: our sons, pride of our Nation, this day have set upon a mighty endeavor, a struggle to preserve our Republic, our religion, and our civilization, and to set free a suffering humanity.[10]

CHAPTER 12

Marshall's Boys at Work

WHEN GEORGE CATLETT MARSHALL BECAME ARMY CHIEF OF STAFF on September 1, 1939, the only generals most Americans could identify were "Black Jack" Pershing and Douglas MacArthur. Hardly anyone in the population of 140 million personally knew a soldier. By June 6, 1944, Americans casually spoke of Ike Eisenhower, Old Blood and Guts Patton, G.I. General Bradley, and Mark Clark as if they were old friends and practically everyone had a relative, friend, or neighbor who was "in the service." The names of obscure places in the Pacific, North Africa, Sicily, and Italy, which few Americans had even heard of before the war, now rolled off a million tongues every day. Since the shock and anger of December 7, 1941, the country had rallied to fight a global war. American troops had rolled the Japanese back across the Pacific, kicked the Germans out of North Africa and Sicily, and stormed into Italy. Now, on D-Day, June 6, 1944, a contingent of soldiers larger than Marshall's entire army in 1939 were hitting Norman beaches with what FDR called an "unconquerable purpose," sure to prevail over "the unholy forces" of the enemy.

The British, Canadian, and French component of the landing force under the command of Bernard Law Montgomery was to drive inland to capture the strategic town of Caen. The Americans were to take Sainte-Mère-Église, then elements of VII Corps were to swing right toward the port of Cherbourg. Once a continuous beachhead had been secured, the entire force would wheel north toward the Seine River to push the Germans out of France and Belgium, then sweep into Germany as the western jaw of a great vise whose eastern jaw was the Red Army. Once Germany was totally defeated, attention would turn to an all-out drive to eliminate the last vestiges of Japan's Empire of the Rising Sun.

From names in his little black book, Marshall had assembled a cadre of commanders on whose shoulders rested the fate of D-Day. Eisenhower was the supreme commander; Omar Bradley commanded the First U.S. Army and would soon assume command of all U.S. forces as the Twelfth Army Group. Marshall's old friend and colleague, Leonard "Gee" Gerow, commanded V Corps, assigned to Omaha Beach. The troops of VII Corps, who landed to the west, on Utah Beach, were under Lightning Joe Collins. Among Collins's intimates was the commander of the Fourth Infantry Division, Major General Raymond Barton, known as Tubby. Attached to Barton's division was one of the most colorful officers in the army, the diminutive Brigadier General Theodore Roosevelt Jr, the oldest son of former president Teddy Roosevelt. Ted Roosevelt, as he was called, had served heroically in World War I, entered government service, ran unsuccessfully for governor of New York against Al Smith, and served as governor general of both Puerto Rico and the Philippines before becoming an executive with book publisher Doubleday. When Japan attacked Pearl Harbor, he appealed to then President Franklin D. Roosevelt to be returned to the army. At fifty-four and seriously crippled by arthritis, he was made a brigadier and deputy to First Division commander Terry de la Mesa Allen in North Africa. At the time, Marshall wrote jokingly to Allen, "T.R. and you are very much of the same type as to enthusiasm. I am a little fearful." Marshall saw Roosevelt as "an A-Number One fighting man with rare courage and what is rarer, unlimited fortitude." He ranked him with Patton as "a favorite swashbuckler."[1]

Going ashore with Roosevelt was Colonel James A. Van Fleet. A West Point classmate of Ike and Bradley, he had been known to Collins as one of the toughest and most versatile backs in an era of fine army football teams.

Collins had also known him at the Infantry School at Fort Benning. "The trouble was," Collins recalled, "that General Marshall, while he served as Assistant Commandant at Benning, confused Van Fleet with a man with almost the same name, for whom Marshall had only slight regard. Although Van Fleet did well over the years, each time during the war when Van Fleet had been recommended to be promoted to the rank of brigadier, Marshall turned him down." It was one of the few times that Marshall's little black book proved fallible. After thoroughly inspecting the Eighth Infantry at their camp in England, Collins called General Bradley and told him they were wasting Van Fleet as a regimental commander. In his opinion, Van Fleet should command a division.

Bradley replied, "Well, Joe, he is in your Corps. Do something about it."

"If Van does as well on D day as I feel sure he will, I will recommend him at once to be a brigadier general," Collins responded.[2] He did, Marshall learned of the case of mistaken identity, and Van Fleet was soon promoted to division and then corps command.

While the American landings on Utah Beach met only light resistance, on Omaha Beach, the invasion did not begin well. After six hours of furious fighting against fierce resistance, the First and Twenty-ninth Divisions remained pinned down. Instead of the "rag-tag static" German troops they had expected to encounter, Bradley explained in his autobiography, "the assault had run head-on into one of Rommel's tough field divisions."[3]

As casualties mounted, Bradley seriously considered abandoning the assault. In a bold and risky maneuver, a squadron of U.S. Navy destroyers risked running aground and taking direct artillery fire from the bluffs. The ships fired salvos that silenced the guns that were decimating the soldiers on Omaha Beach and freed the troops to scale the bluffs. The beach was finally taken at a cost of 1,465 dead and 5,000 wounded or missing.

By nightfall, the Allied forces in Normandy totaled 165,000, more than eight divisions. Although Marshall had no immediate role in the tactical planning and execution of the landings, he had chosen those who did the work. Thanks to the training of the mostly conscripted citizen army he had organized; thanks to his modernization of that army into one of swift battlefield maneuverability, with an amphibious and airborne capability; thanks to his creation of an efficient staff bureaucracy; and thanks to his vision of unified command under a single supreme commander, the U.S.

Army led the greatest invasion in history, cracked Hitler's vaunted "Atlantic Wall" in a single day, and stood poised to sweep toward Germany and victory in Europe.

+===+

Unwilling to remain in Washington remote from the action, on June 8, Marshall, Hap Arnold, and Admiral Ernest J. King boarded an army C–54 and flew to Great Britain to confer with Eisenhower at his forward headquarters south of London. After a briefing on June 9 by the British Chiefs of Staff, and a conference with Churchill the next day, they met Eisenhower at Portsmouth, crossed the Channel on a destroyer, switched to a landing craft, and landed on Omaha Beach. They visited a group of wounded waiting to be evacuated to England, then traveled to Bradley's command post in an apple orchard, where Generals Gerow, Courtney Hodges, and Collins briefed them on the landings.

Satisfied by his firsthand tour of the early phase of the invasion effort, Marshall returned to London and cabled Roosevelt that he found Eisenhower and Bradley cool and confident while carrying out a plan of incredible magnitude and complication with superlative efficiency.

Marshall did not deceive himself that he was in the thick of the action. True, Omaha Beach on D-Day plus 2 was a lot closer to the war than his office in the Pentagon, but it was still D-Day *plus 2*. His stay in London proved more interesting. Not only were there Hitler's V–1 rockets to contend with, there was also the self-appointed leader of the Free French, Charles de Gaulle. Both Eisenhower and Bradley complained bitterly about the Frenchman's lack of cooperation, which was founded on his belief that he should have a major leadership role in the invasion. Marshall was outraged. He had no objection to de Gaulle's becoming the de facto head of the French government, but he was deeply concerned that his refusal to subordinate himself to Eisenhower as supreme commander would undermine the success of the invasion. President Roosevelt had directed Marshall to avoid talking politics when he was in England, but when Britain's foreign secretary, Anthony Eden, defended de Gaulle, Marshall quietly informed him that "no sons of Iowa farmers would fight to put statues of de Gaulle in France."[4] He went on to warn Eden that de Gaulle's misbehavior could create a destructive wave of indignation among the American people.

De Gaulle's countryman Napoleon Bonaparte had once famously proclaimed enemies to be bad, but allies even worse. Marshall could sympathize. Not only did he find himself confronting de Gaulle's intransigence, he was now subjected by the British chiefs of staff to an argument in favor of abandoning Operation Anvil—the proposed invasion of southern France—in order to concentrate on the faltering conquest of Italy and a subsequent drive into the Balkans and Austria. Marshall had feared that the Italian adventure would come to this, and he now stood his ground, making the counterargument that seizing the Mediterranean ports of Marseilles and Toulon was vital to the invasion for three reasons. First, it secured a line of communication, reinforcement, and supply to keep the invasion going. Second, it maintained a line of retreat, if one were needed. Third, it prevented the Germans from counterattacking from the rear.

In part to bolster his advocacy of Operation Anvil, Marshall took flight in a small plane from London by way of Algiers and over Salerno to Anzio and thence to Rome. He wanted to assess the Italian front for himself and to personally debrief Fifth Army commander Mark Clark. He also had a strong desire to visit his stepson's grave at Anzio.

After visiting the Anzio cemetery where Allen Brown had been buried among the 7,000 men who perished there, Marshall flew on to Rome, where he met Clark. The Fifth Army commander made an earnest plea for further immediate action in northern Italy, and he backed the British Balkan strategy. Marshall, however, ordered him to go no farther than the Apennine Mountains, and explained that, regardless of what the British might say, the war was to be won in France, not in Italy, and that the second invasion, of southern France, was the priority. It was hard to deny a commander in a bloody fight all that he wanted, but seeing the big picture and balancing one objective against another was the essence of Marshall's job as Marshall himself saw it.

Operation Anvil had been delayed and was now called Operation Dragoon, partly because of fears that the original code name had been compromised and partly because a reluctant Winston Churchill complained that he had been "dragooned" into agreeing to the operation. The invasion of southern France was commanded by Lieutenant General Alexander Patch, with ground troops under Major General Lucian Truscott. Accompanied by a contingent of Free French forces, Truscott's army landed in the Cannes-Toulon region on August 15, 1944, and established a fifty-mile bridgehead by the end of the first day. French resistance fighters, the so-called Maquis, took the ports of Marseilles and Toulon two weeks later. Truscott's troops advanced northward to link up with the newly created Third Army, led by Patton. This, however, depended on Patton and the rest of what was now Bradley's Twelfth Army Group breaking out of the Norman hedgerow country. To effect this, Bradley drew up Operation Cobra, which was to begin with massive bombardment of German positions to be followed by an attack by Collins' VII Corps. The area to be bombed was a rectangle 7,000 yards wide and 5,000 yards deep south of the Perriers-St. Lo Road. Cobra called for Collins's troops to pull back about a mile just before the bombing. It was tactically complex and risky.

On the day the air armada took off, July 24, the weather over the target area was so miserable that British air commander Leigh Mallory postponed the attack and recalled the bombers. More than 300 heavy bombers did not receive the recall order and proceeded with the attack. Instead of flying perpendicular to the road, according to the plan, they had come in parallel to it, with the tragic result that some of their bombs rained down on the Americans, killing 25 men of the Thirtieth Division and leaving 131 wounded. Compounding this loss was the fact that, in pulling back from the area under bombardment, the Americans had relinquished some territory and had to fight hard to regain it, an effort that resulted in 77 Thirty-ninth Infantry casualties, among them their much respected commander, Colonel Paddy Flint, who was killed. Yet worse were the results of a second air attack on July 25, when bombs once again fell short, this time killing 61 and wounding 374 men of the Thirtieth Division. The Forty-seventh Infantry Regiment of the Ninth Division had 14 dead and 33 wounded, bringing total VII Corps casualties to friendly fire to 601, including 111 killed. Among the dead on July 25 was Lieutenant General Leslie J. McNair, the officer who had implemented much of the training policy Marshall had championed. Of necessity a desk soldier, he had decided to join an assault battalion on this occasion to see the bombing firsthand.[5]

Profoundly depressed by the friendly fire casualties, Bradley despaired of the success of Operation Cobra, but soon learned that the air attack had indeed been devastating to the enemy. Collins received intelligence reports that the German defensive positions had been churned into mounds of earth, under which hundreds of Germans had been buried alive. Dazed prisoners babbled about the hell that the bombs had made of a key road and a command post. Nevertheless, the ground attack by the Fourth, Ninth, and Thirtieth Divisions met dogged resistance from the infantry of the Panzer Lehr Division and troops of the German Fifth Parachute Division. Having already been hit by friendly bombs, the Thirtieth Division found itself strafed by British fighter-bombers and checked by British Mark V tanks, but still managed to make progress.

While fighting raged in and around the town of Marigny for two days, Second Armored, the Thirtieth Division, and General Maurice Rose's combat team A reached St. Gilles in the middle of the afternoon, rolled through it, and opened the exploitation phase of Cobra. After a fight that Collins termed "some of the wildest melees" of the war, VII Corps was directed in Bradley's Field Orders No. 2 to continue operations to isolate enemy forces and at the same time continue pushing rapidly to the south.

In the midst of the early Cobra action, Eisenhower sent Marshall notification of McNair's death. It arrived just two weeks after a report that Brigadier General Ted Roosevelt had died suddenly of a heart attack on the night of July 11. Pending transmission to Marshall from Eisenhower on the very night he died was a recommendation that he be promoted to Major General and given command of a division. He was buried in Normandy on July 14, with six generals as honorary pallbearers, including his boss in the Fourth Division on D-Day, "Tubby" Barton, Collins, Patton, and Bradley. Ike recommended, and Marshall approved, awarding him the Medal of Honor for his leadership on Utah Beach. Congress ratified it unanimously. It was presented to his wife, Eleanor, on September 22, 1944, at the White House, by President Roosevelt.

One week after the launching of Cobra, Marshall sent a cable to Eisenhower noting that the Washington representative of the British chiefs of staff had complained about a lack of knowledge "concerning your plans and your estimate of the situation." Marshall added that he himself was also in the dark in regards to Eisenhower's "thoughts concerning the situation" and probable course of action. "For instance," Marshall specified, "we received no information of Bradley's present offensive except an unexplained reference in a radio [message] from [Secretary of War] Stimson referring to Cobra, whatever that was."

In one of the most detailed replies he'd ever given to Marshall, a chastened Eisenhower apologized on August 2 for not having kept him "more fully abreast of future plans." He explained Cobra as an effort to break through "such reinforcements as [the enemy] can gather from within France . . . . We are attacking viciously in an effort to accomplish our purpose before the enemy can be successful in establishing new and strong lines. . . . I am very hopeful as to immediate results, and believe that within the next two or three days we will so manhandle the western flank of the enemy's forces that we will secure for ourselves freedom of action through destruction of a considerable portion of the forces facing us."[6]

Five days after Marshall received this estimate, Eisenhower was at Bradley's headquarters in France as the Germans launched a counterattack in the region of the town of Mortain. What their commander, General Gunther von Kluge, the German high command in Berlin, and Hitler did not know was that Eisenhower and Bradley were (as Eisenhower later wrote in *Crusade in Europe*) "aware that the German counterattack was in preparation." Because the Allies had come into possession of one of Germany's "Enigma" encoding and decoding machines early in the war and had figured out how it worked, they often read orders from Berlin to field commanders before they reached the hands of Hitler's own generals. Believing that Mortain could be defended with a minimum of forces, Bradley decided to rush troops south and east to begin an envelopment of the German spearheads, with Patton's Third Army sweeping north. To complete the formation of this trap, Montgomery's Second Army and a Canadian force were to drive south from the Caen region in the direction of the town of Falaise to link up with the Americans at Argentan to close the net.

"With the great bulk of all Allied forces attacking from the perimeter of a great half-circle toward a common center," Eisenhower noted later, "the determination of the exact points on which each element would halt, in order not to become involved against friendly units coming from the opposite direction, was a tricky problem."[7]

Fresh in everyone's memory were those hundreds of Americans killed by errant bombs. Because the only way to prevent a similar friendly fire disaster was by halting the converging Allies before they mistakenly clashed, Bradley did so. Patton favored taking a greater risk in order to bag as many of the enemy as possible and cut off their line of retreat, but Bradley later explained that he preferred "a solid shoulder at Argentan than the possibility of a broken neck at Falaise."[8]

While the Allies avoided what Eisenhower felt might have been "a calamitous battle between friends," the Germans fought desperately to hold open the mouth of the closing pocket, known as "the Falaise Gap," and therefore managed the withdrawal of what Ike called "a disappointing portion" of their Panzer tanks—although two Panzer divisions and eight infantry divisions were captured almost in their entirety. Surveying the aftermath of the Falaise battle two days after the fighting stopped, Ike was horrified by one of the worst "killing grounds" of the war, on which it was possible to walk for hundreds of yards at a time, stepping on nothing but dead and decaying flesh.

Thanks in large part to Patton's vigorous drive across France, Operation Cobra was expanded from a breakout into a general eastward advance. As the remnants of the German army in France were in retreat across the Seine River on August 25, 1944, Paris was liberated, with the Second French Armored Division, part of the U.S. First Army, given the honor of leading the way into the city.

Marshall felt that the expansion of Cobra and the liberation of Paris amply vindicated his absolute insistence on carrying out Operation Dragoon. Opening a second line of advance in the south of France had been essential to the success of the invasion. Churchill continued to protest the withdrawal of troops from Italy, but Marshall continued to stand firm, and President Roosevelt enthusiastically backed him up. Eisenhower, Bradley, Patton, and their subordinates had to fight the enemy on the ground, but Marshall had to tangle with America's British ally at the highest level yet without undermining the alliance on which so much still depended. It was a balancing act requiring tremendous strength and utmost delicacy. Historians justly give Eisenhower credit for making the difficult Anglo-American alliance work, but while Ike, headquartered in England and France, was the front man of the alliance, its operation depended just as much on Marshall back in Washington. He had the unenviable task of acting in the best interests of the alliance while also consistently backing his commanders. This meant convincing the British that his decisions did not automatically favor Americans while simultaneously persuading his subordinates that he was not knuckling under to the British.

By September 5, ninety days after D-Day, more than two million Allied troops and 3,446,000 tons of stores had been put ashore in France. Even for Marshall, the man who had forged a reputation in World War I as a master at moving large numbers of men and shifting supplies, this was a stunning logistical achievement. But Marshall did not rest on his laurels. His *Biennial Report* through June 1944 contained his warning that much more in the way of supplies was needed to support "the fast moving offensive across France" even as the Germans were "heading for the shelter of the Siegfried Line."[9]

Supply was looming as the choke point for the invasion, and it would continue to occupy Marshall through to the end. Nevertheless, during the third week of September 1944, he was again in conference in Quebec with Roosevelt and Churchill, joining them in the triumphant face they now put upon the war. Everyone took pains to project perfect agreement among the Allies. If Churchill was still bitter over drawing resources from Italy to feed Operation Dragoon, he did not let on, telling reporters that the conference was held in "a blaze of friendship."[10]

On the agenda were Britain's role in the Pacific war after the defeat of Germany; how the Pacific command would be split between MacArthur and Admiral Chester Nimitz; whether the next big Pacific campaign should be aimed at retaking the Philippines to fulfill MacArthur's promise to return, or should be an assault on the island of Formosa as a stepping-stone to Japan (as Nimitz preferred); and how to divide zones of occupation in Germany between the Allies. Supply, supply, supply was uppermost in Marshall's thoughts as the European invasion continued. But, in a momentous conference that was less military than political, he had to hold his logistical concerns in abeyance as he found himself called upon to think less like a soldier and more like a statesman as the prospect of victory raised the specter of the people of Europe struggling to rise out of the ruin and want of war, while their leaders chewed over old rivalries and resurrected issues of national interests and colonial aspirations. Hard as the logistical puzzle was, the diplomatic and humanitarian crises he could see coming appeared both vast and well-nigh intractable. But he had come too far to seek refuge in the protests that these were not a humble soldier's province. At the second Quebec conference, more than ever before, George Marshall saw his future and the future of "military" command that could never again be purely military.

CHAPTER 13

"We Can Still Lose This War"

WHILE FRANKLIN D. ROOSEVELT BEGAN HIS CAMPAIGN FOR ELECTION to a fourth term, running against New York Republican governor Thomas E. Dewey, Marshall chose to visit Eisenhower in Paris and the generals on the front lines. Traveling with him on the first Army Air Transport plane to fly nonstop from New York to Paris were Assistant Chief of Staff for Operations Thomas Handy and Director of War Mobilization James F. Byrnes, a former congressman, senator, U.S. Supreme Court justice, and future secretary of state. Eisenhower, Bradley, and Eisenhower's chief of staff, Walter Bedell Smith, met them at Le Bourget Field on August 6, 1944. A little more than an hour later, a War Department courier arrived at Quarters No. 1 at Fort Myer to present Katherine Marshall with another innovation: the first-ever radio-telephoto transmitted from Europe to the United States. It showed her husband and Ike on the airport tarmac, shaking hands and smiling.

Conferring in Ike's office in a small white stone annex behind the stately Trianon Palace Hotel—quarters Ike deemed too extravagant for him—Marshall expressed his concerns, the most pressing of which were supplies and manpower. The invasion forces had failed to secure adequate seaport facilities to keep pace with the ground troops' eastward progress. Although ample supplies of ammunition and gasoline were being off-loaded in Cherbourg and other Atlantic ports, transporting them overland to the forces that were advancing daily farther from the ports was becoming an increasingly critical problem. Patton and his Third Army had to be halted more than once for want of fuel. Moreover, the American public, suffering from what Eisenhower and others called "victory fever," was becoming increasingly resistant to additional call-ups of men for a war they believed was all but won. Marshall was forced to direct Eisenhower to strip rear echelons of clerks, cooks, and other support personnel to replenish frontline forces. In effect, every soldier was to be considered a rifleman.

Urgent as the logistical and manpower problems were, they were nothing new to Marshall, who had handled similar predicaments in World War I. He found it less easy to manage the public and press uproar in Great Britain over how Eisenhower's appointment to supreme command of Allied operations had relegated Montgomery, whom the British public revered as their greatest war hero since Lord Wellington, to what they—and the egocentric Monty himself—saw as a humiliatingly subordinate role. At the same time, Patton, Bradley, and other top American ground commanders were outraged over what they felt was Ike's willingness to subordinate *them* to Monty. Certainly, Eisenhower was apportioning the lion's share of gasoline and other supplies to his army group. Finally, Bradley, always a realist, had just informed Marshall that earlier predictions of an end to the war by Christmas of 1944 were far too optimistic. Now Marshall had to face manning and supplying a war effort that was likely to stretch longer than anyone had thought. The early dark days of the war had been dangerous indeed, but the days of brighter hopes brought their own dangers: the consequences of premature assumptions of victory.

On October 8, Marshall and Bradley flew through thick fog to General Montgomery's headquarters in Brussels. Three weeks earlier, Montgomery had launched Operation Market-Garden, an Anglo-American airborne assault deep into the enemy's rear areas in conjunction with a ground attack by the British Second Army with the objective of forcing a Rhine crossing earlier than anyone—especially the Germans—had expected. Montgomery's idea was to inject paratroops along a thin corridor approximately eighty miles into Holland from Eindhoven northward to Arnhem. They were to secure bridges across several canals, as well as across three major water barriers, including the main downstream branch of the Rhine. The principal objectives were to get Allied troops across the Rhine, cut off any German forces remaining in western Holland, outflank the enemy's frontier defenses (the so-called West Wall, or Siegfried Line, Hitler's last-ditch defense against an invasion of Germany from the west), and position the British ground forces for a full-scale drive into Germany.

The largest airborne drop in military history, Market-Garden involved three divisions. The U.S. 101st Airborne would drop on Eindhoven and take canal crossings at Veghel. The U.S. Eighty-second Airborne would land on bridges over the Maas and the Waal Rivers, sixty miles behind the German lines, and connect with the British First Airborne and a Polish Airborne Brigade. As it turned out, except for the Eighty-second Airborne, all forces deployed were unable to achieve their objectives. Units were dropped in the wrong places and were cut off, with one actually landing *on* part of a Panzer division. Out of the 10,000 men dropped around Arnhem, 1,400 were killed and more than 6,000 were taken prisoner.

While Eisenhower had thought the plan a fair gamble, Bradley had strenuously objected to it, arguing that by attempting to force a Rhine crossing on a very narrow front, Montgomery was departing from the agreed-upon Allied strategy of advancing into Germany across a broad front, which would result in far more sustainable gains. Unabashed by the failure of Market-Garden, Field Marshal Montgomery, who could not tolerate Allied officers who argued against him, complained to Marshall at Brussels that since Eisenhower had taken personal command of the land battle, the armies had become separated by nationality and not geography. "There was a lack of grip, and operational direction and control were lacking," he asserted. "Our operations had, in fact, become ragged and disjointed, and we had got ourselves into a real mess."

Even as he had to struggle against some of his own commanders, who complained that Eisenhower (at Marshall's direction) had taken the unified command concept too far by knuckling under to the British, Marshall was now hearing from the top British commander in Europe that unified command had broken down. It was an indictment of Eisenhower, the very man whom Marshall had plucked from obscurity and elevated to the pinnacle of authority in the Mediterranean and European theaters and, even more, an indictment of Marshall as the advocate of unified command and the architect of the coalition of forces known as the Allies. Marshall struggled to keep himself from "blowing off out of turn" and to suppress a strong impulse to "whittle" Montgomery down. "And then I thought," Marshall recalled, "now this is Eisenhower's business and not mine, and I had better not meddle, though it was very hard for me to restrain myself because I didn't think there was any logic in what [Montgomery] had said but overwhelming egotism."[1] Thus Marshall resolved to do the hardest thing for a senior commander to do: forgo the impulse to micromanage a difficult situation and instead trust his deputy to find a way to carry out his directives. It was a mark of Marshall's maturity that he had learned to adopt restraint as a key component of his leadership of the war. The hallmark of Marshall as a military executive had always been the genius that guided him to put the right man in the right spot. The corollary of this was the trust he placed in the judgment of the men he chose. This principle—choose the right people for the job, then get out of their way and let them do it—is among the leading lessons in leadership Marshall bequeathed to the American military. And yet, in the postwar American military, it has been a lesson more often honored in the breach than the observance. A long line of conflicts, from Vietnam through Operation Restore Hope and its aftermath in Somalia (1992–1994) and the wars in Afghanistan (2001-) and Iraq (2003-), have suffered from high-level micromanagement and a mixture of inability and unwillingness to formulate clear policy and unambiguous objectives and then to entrust their execution to commanders on the ground.

After a week of visiting five army, eight corps, and sixteen division headquarters, greeting the staffs of eight other divisions, and talking to scores of GIs, Marshall flew back to Washington on October 16 to find Roosevelt pushing a bill in Congress to create a five-star rank, equivalent to Europe's field marshal, to be conferred on MacArthur, Eisenhower, Arnold, and admirals Leahy,

King, Nimitz, and Halsey—and himself. Marshall was opposed to the bill because he did not want to feel "beholden to Congress" when he went to Capitol Hill to seek approval of his requests for legislation. Marshall also believed that awarding these five-star ranks diminished the honor given to John J. Pershing after World War I and, in the end, he succeeded in persuading Congress to preserve the title "general of the *armies*" for Pershing alone while designating the five-star rank as "general of the *army*," singular. The new rank was conferred on Marshall in a ceremony at the Pentagon on December 15, 1944. At virtually the same time, Congress voted to waive the army's regulation requiring him to retire on December 31, when he reached the age sixty-four.

Eisenhower received word of his own promotion to five-star rank on December 16. In the two months since Marshall's visit, Allied forces in France and Belgium had settled into winter positions from Holland to the Swiss border. By mid-December, Bradley had become so alarmed by the manpower shortage that he asked Eisenhower for permission to send a representative to the Pentagon to try to straighten out the problem. "Not only had Washington juggled our quotas to shortchange us on infantrymen," Bradley noted, "but in November at a time our requirements increased, the War Department cut back our monthly allotment of replacements from 80,000 to 67,000 men. At the very moment we needed them most, too many men were being diverted to the Pacific."

Bradley complained to Ike, "Don't they realize that we can still lose this war in Europe?"[2]

"They"—meaning George Marshall—did realize it, but his supremely difficult job was to see beyond the confines of a single theater in this two-theater war. Even though Japan was suffering one defeat after another, its military leaders showed no sign of surrendering. Resistance had turned suicidal, and in facing defeat the Japanese army and navy were taking a heavier toll on American forces than they had in the early days of the war, when Japan was victorious. Indeed, Japan's only hope for averting total defeat was to outlast the American will to continue the fight. For this reason, Marshall had to devote as much manpower to the Pacific as possible. From the perspective of the commanders in Europe, this was a terrible mistake. From that of the Pacific leaders, it was an action long overdue. Early in the war, it had been a matter of policy to see to the defeat of Germany before opening an offensive against Japan. For Marshall, this was a difficult enough position to be in. If anything, however, that position was even more difficult as the war in Europe drew to a close. For now, policy was less definite and required that the chief of staff make, on an ongoing basis, very difficult manpower decisions—and to make them at a time when the American people wanted their "boys" to come back home, when war funds were running low, and when no one in government wanted to add substantially to an army that would soon have to be demobilized.

Although Marshall had to balance two theaters, Bradley's fears about the possibility of still losing the war were well founded. Preparatory to an all-out offensive on the Western Front, Eisenhower had deployed troops over a broad area so that the advance could be made at several points simultaneously. This disposition left the Ardennes Forest region of Belgium very thinly defended. The sector, after all, had been quiet since its fateful eruption at the start of the Battle of France in 1940. Only four divisions of Bradley's Twelfth Army Group, a mixture of green recruits and battle-weary veterans, guarded a seventy-five-mile front. This presented German general Gerd von Rundstedt with an extraordinary opportunity to execute an order that had come directly from Adolf Hitler. Having barely escaped an attempt on his life by army officers in July 1944, Hitler told officers at his daily briefing on September 16, "I have just made a momentous decision. I shall go over to the counterattack out of the Ardennes, with the objective of driving to Antwerp."

Of the plan, codenamed *Wacht am Rehin* ("Watch on the Rhine"), von Rundstedt wrote, "I was staggered. It was obvious to me that the available forces were too small for such an extremely ambitious plan." But now Eisenhower and Bradley had given von Rundstedt an unexpected opening. In the first two weeks of December, 1,500 trains carrying troops, armor, and artillery unloaded in secrecy in rail yards east of the Ardennes. In the last three nights before the offensive was to start, a quarter of a million men, 717 tanks and assault guns, and 2,623 heavy artillery pieces were in position less than four miles from under-strength American divisions. The Führer told the generals of the gathering force, "This battle will determine whether we live or die," and von Rundstedt rallied his troops with the exhortation, "Soldiers of the Western Front! Your great hour has arrived." Every one of them, he said, bore "a holy obligation to give everything to achieve things beyond human possibilities for our Fatherland and our Führer!"[3]

On December 16, 1944, Omar Bradley hitched a ride with Brigadier General Joseph James O'Hare, who was about to set off on a trip to the Pentagon to hash out the manpower issue. While O'Hare would go on to Paris, Bradley's destination was Eisenhower's headquarters at Versailles. The next afternoon, a colonel entered the conference room and handed a note to Ike's intelligence chief. British Major General Kenneth Strong read it and interrupted the meeting to announce that at five o'clock that morning the Germans had attacked at five points in Belgium.

General Walter Bedell Smith put a hand on Bradley's shoulder and said, "Well, Brad, you've been wishing for a counterattack. Now it looks as though you've got it."

"A counterattack yes," said Bradley, "but I'll be damned if I wanted one this big."[4]

In fact, the Ardennes Offensive, which developed into the Battle of the Bulge, the biggest and costliest battle the American army fought in Europe, threatened to become a catastrophe. Both Bradley and Eisenhower had been caught by surprise, though both rose to the occasion and, thanks in large measure to Patton and this Third Army, turned imminent disaster into a counteroffensive that broke the back of the German army, ending its capacity to ever again mount another offensive.

Through it all, George C. Marshall resisted all temptation to interfere. When Colonel George Lincoln of the Operations Division came to him with suggestions about units that could be moved to reinforce the beleaguered Ardennes forces, Marshall cut him off. "We can't help Eisenhower in any way other than not bothering him. No messages will go from here to the ETO unless approved by me."[5] Yet again, the chief of staff demonstrated the extraordinary power of self-restraint. Only Eisenhower, Bradley, Patton, and the other commanders, officers, and men at the front were capable of determining the outcome of the battle. This being the case, it was time for the chief of staff to remain silent.

But there would be a limit to the silence.

On Christmas Day, the sky over the Belgian town of Bastogne cleared, allowing Allied bombers to attack, and on December 26 units of Patton's Third Army reached the Bastogne perimeter. The 101st Airborne and Tenth Armored Division, which had been surrounded there, were about to be rescued. Eisenhower, Patton, and Bradley wanted to do more than effect a rescue, and Bradley put forth a plan for a full-scale counterattack. An enthusiastic Eisenhower urged Montgomery to commit all his forces to it, but Monty not only rejected the plan, he demanded that Eisenhower turn Bradley's troops over to him. He also launched into a blistering public indictment of both Eisenhower and Bradley for having allowed themselves to be taken by surprise. The British press trumpeted accounts of the Battle of the Bulge that credited the United Kingdom with winning it and demanded that Montgomery be given command of all ground forces.

For Eisenhower, champion of unified command, it was finally too much. He drafted a cable to the Combined Chiefs of Staff demanding that they choose between him and Montgomery. Now Marshall broke his silence. He sent Ike a cable advising him "under no circumstances [to] make any concessions of any kind whatsoever" to Montgomery or anyone else. "You not only have our complete confidence," Marshall continued, "but there would be a terrific resentment in this country following such action."[6]

When Eisenhower showed Montgomery's chief of staff the message he intended to send to the Combined Chiefs, he also presented the cable he had received from Marshall. This prompted Monty's man to plead with Ike to delay sending his cable to the Combined Chiefs of Staff for a day, during which time the aide flew to London and warned Montgomery that it was "in the cards that you might have to go." Stunned, Montgomery backed down and sent Ike an apology. Knowing that he wielded tremendous influence, Marshall always husbanded it carefully, so that when he did finally exercise it, his word had a force before which even a supreme egoist like Montgomery gave way.

Marshall had saved Eisenhower. Had Eisenhower yielded command to Montgomery, the senior commanders of the American army would surely have rebelled. Some might have resigned their commissions—both Bradley and Patton threatened to—and, at the very least, both unity of command and the Anglo-American alliance would have been seriously undermined. In saving Eisenhower, Marshall had saved the grand alliance of the war. And now, with the Battle of the Bulge having been turned into an Allied victory, the heart of Germany lay open to the forces led by Eisenhower—not Bernard Law Montgomery. For Marshall, this momentous turn of events would mean yet another great conference to attend, this one, for the first time in the war, on Russian soil.

CHAPTER 14

Warrior Statesman

ON THE LAST DAY OF 1944, GENERAL HAP ARNOLD ORGANIZED A small surprise party to celebrate George Marshall's sixty-fourth birthday. Secretary of War Stimson began his toast with a passage from the Book of Proverbs: "He who controlleth his spirit is better than he who taketh a city." He concluded by saying, "It has been a great privilege to have been associated with you and I devoutly hope that you will continue your leadership until victory is achieved."[1]

These were gracious remarks from a man with whom Marshall had clashed over the war secretary's proposal for an accelerated draft to create ten divisions by the fall of 1945 for a projected invasion of the Japanese homeland. A realist who had devoted much of his military career—that is, his entire adult life—to training and professional education, Marshall argued that it took two years to train a division. Further, he pointed out that Stimson's plan would mean "robbing us terribly" of men needed at home for critical civilian industries. Just as Marshall had to balance the needs of the Pacific theater against the European, so he had to balance the combat theaters against the home front, the vital center of war production. He was so opposed to Stimson's plan that he asked the secretary to tell President Roosevelt he was on "the point of resigning."[2]

Stimson backed down.

During the Battle of the Bulge, Eisenhower's seventy-three divisions had been depleted by 77,000 men, most of them infantry. Since D-Day, the casualty toll was half a million, with 90,000 killed. Although Army Intelligence estimated that the Germans had lost a quarter of a million, including 36,000 taken prisoner, in the Ardennes campaign alone, they still had seventy divisions left to defend their homeland, with the broad and mighty Rhine River standing in the way of the Allies.

In the Pacific, MacArthur's forces had moved to the Philippines. By December 1, 1944, seven divisions were well established ashore on the island of Leyte, five airfields were operating, and the U.S. Navy dominated the surrounding waters.

On January 20, 1945, George and Katherine Marshall were up early in Quarters No. 1 at Fort Myer so that he could go to his office in the Pentagon before joining her at a 10 A.M. religious service at the White House and the noontime swearing-in of Franklin D. Roosevelt for his fourth term as president. Because of bitterly cold weather and Roosevelt's frail health, the ceremony had been moved from the east front of the Capitol to the South Portico of the White House to spare the president the inaugural procession and to provide some shelter from the elements. Katherine described Roosevelt as "pale and drawn," his hands trembling and his voice weak. "It was tragic to see the havoc the past four years had wrought," she wrote. "The handwriting on the wall was unmistakable, despite all denials on the part of those surrounding him."[3]

Taking the oath first was Roosevelt's new vice president, Senator Harry S. Truman of Missouri. Replacing Henry Wallace—vice president during FDR's third term, whose left-leaning views had grown excessively controversial—Truman had created and chaired a Special Committee to Investigate the National Defense Program (Seventy-seventh and Seventy-eighth Congresses), the so-called Truman Committee that rooted out corruption and inefficiency among military contractors. It was during his service on this committee, Truman later recalled for biographer Merle Miller, that he first "got to know General Marshall really well, and I got to know that you could depend on every word he said, that he just never would lie to you, and that he always knew what he was talking about."[4]

＋＞—·—＜＋

As Truman took the office that Roosevelt's first vice president, John Nance Garner, had said was "not worth a bucket of warm piss," Marshall possessed a secret denied to almost everyone in government, including Truman. Since 1939, the United States had been exploring the possibility of building a bomb based on splitting the uranium or plutonium atom. In 1942 the so-called Manhattan Engineer District—or Manhattan Project—was set up under the command of Brigadier General Leslie Groves, who had just finished directing construction of the Pentagon. In December 1944, Groves was able to report to Roosevelt, Stimson, and Marshall that one atomic bomb would be ready by August 1, 1945, and another by year's end. The weapon had yet to be tested, but, assuming it worked, it would give the United States the greatest destructive force ever devised. Work on the bomb had been undertaken out of fear that Hitler's scientists were on the verge of developing a nuclear weapon. As Germany slipped inexorably toward defeat, Japan loomed as the bomb's target. A weapon so terrible might be just the thing to coerce the Empire's surrender, thereby saving the lives of tens of thousands of American soldiers who would otherwise have to invade Japan, and at the same time making the entrance of the Soviet Union into the Pacific war unnecessary—thereby reducing the chances that Japan would come under the Soviet sphere of influence.

In February 1945, no one yet knew whether the atomic bomb would actually work. Some, among them Admiral William D. Leahy, the president's chief of staff, doubted it would prove more than scientific theory. Thus Roosevelt and Churchill traveled to the Crimean resort city of Yalta to confer with Stalin on the final phase of the war with Germany and, assuming the bomb would not become a reality, to set a date for Soviet entry into the war with Japan. En route to Yalta by sea, Roosevelt and Churchill planned to rendezvous on the island of Malta to coordinate military and political strategies for dealing with both issues. Before joining the two leaders there, Marshall intended to confer with Eisenhower in Marseilles, France, on the plan to end the European war by crushing as much of the German army west of the Rhine as possible, then crossing the river in force.

Marshall also planned to squelch a renewed demand by the British for shared command. He believed, as did Roosevelt, that in the commitment of men, casualties suffered, and sacrifices of the American people in producing the guns, ammunition, tanks, planes, and ships for the liberation of Europe, the United States had earned not only the right to dictate terms of the military endgame, but to claim the dominant role in the political, economic, and military future of postwar Europe. It was Marshall's view that the United States must not repeat the mistake it had made after World War I by withdrawing from Europe. Woodrow Wilson had cast the United States in the role of democracy's defender, but an isolationist Republican Congress that dominated his second term and the isolationist Republican president who succeeded him in office largely withdrew America from the world stage. Further, Marshall perceived that without the strong presence of the United States in global affairs following the Great War, Marshall believed, Germany, Italy, and Japan were able to make a *second* world war inevitable. This time, in arranging a postwar order, Marshall wanted to ensure that the United States acted on the principles Wilson had set forth. He could not have known at the time that he, as secretary of state under Truman, would himself become a leader of that action, but even at the start of 1945, as army chief of staff, he knew that he was boldly entering into global affairs and helping to bring the nation along with him.

The precedents for global leadership that Marshall was instrumental in creating have influenced American presidents and other leaders in crafting foreign policy during the Cold War and after. Yet whereas during most of the half-century that followed World War II, America's leading role in global affairs was widely accepted both at home and abroad, bitter experiences in Vietnam, Iraq, and Afghanistan have increasingly called this brand of foreign policy into question, leaving us to speculate whether the age of Marshall and his kind is fading or has already vanished altogether.

In stormy conferences at Malta with the British chiefs of staff over Eisenhower's plan for crossing the Rhine, shifting some U.S. troops from Italy to Ike's command, and over how to conduct the final phase of the Pacific war, Marshall was implacable in asserting the position of the United States that

World War II would end on America's terms. What Europe and the rest of the globe would look like politically thereafter would be determined at Yalta by Roosevelt, Churchill, and Stalin.

In their first meeting at Yalta, which Roosevelt chaired, Marshall delivered an extemporaneous summary of the Allied situation that Churchill called brilliantly concise and Roosevelt's new secretary of state, Edward R. Stettinius Jr., described as one of the most magnificent presentations he had ever heard. After this, however, Marshall found himself more an observer of the proceedings than a participant as the Big Three simply agreed to leave Allied military strategy and tactics against Germany entirely up to Eisenhower. They also agreed on dividing Berlin and Germany into zones of occupation, with Berlin a zoned enclave in the heart of the Soviet zone. They further settled on British and Russian spheres of influence around the globe, and then bargained over Stalin's demands that he be given Japanese territory for getting into the Pacific war.

Having attained Big Three endorsement of the American plan for invading Germany, Marshall flew from Yalta to Italy to confer with General Mark Clark about the interminable Italian campaign, which Congresswoman Clare Booth Luce had provocatively described as "the forgotten front." Wife of *Life* and *Time* magazine publisher Henry Luce, she had been taken on a tour of the front at Christmastime by General Lucian Truscott, and *Life* had published a long article, profusely illustrated with photographs of weary, muddy GIs, under the subtitle "U.S. Fifth Army Fights a Plodding War in Italy." As he toured the front, Marshall was followed by a swarm of reporters, drawn to Italy by the Luce criticism of the campaign and attracted by the presence of the army chief of staff. Marshall, of course, had opposed devoting so many resources to the Italian campaign, and had he been a commander of lesser character, he might well have taken steps to distance himself from it. But he understood that, while he had been right to have fought vigorously for the strategic ends in which he believed, once the decision had been made nevertheless to commit to a major campaign in Italy, his role was to manage and support it to the best of his ability. Far from trying to put distance between himself and the heartbreaking campaign, he was determined to show Clark and his men that they were not "forgotten" and that he believed the Italian campaign—which he had opposed—was now a crucial component in the defeat of Germany. To the reporters in his wake, he calmly pointed out that the

Allies were fighting a global war and tying down some twenty-seven German divisions in Italy was an extraordinary achievement, whether or not it made headlines. As a demonstration of his solidarity with the Fifth Army, Marshall spent three days in Italy, as close to an active front line as he had been in France as General Pershing's operations officer in 1918.

On his return to the Pentagon, Marshall received a message from the man who had pressed him to open an Italian front in the first place. Winston Churchill sent a cable via the British military chief in Washington that said, "Pray give General Marshall my warmest congratulations on the magnificent fighting and conduct of the American and Allied armies under General Eisenhower, and say what a joy it must be to him to see how the armies he called into being by his own genius have won immortal renown. He is the true organizer of victory."[5]

At the end of February 1945, seven field armies, consisting of four million men, three-quarters of them American, in 53 infantry and 20 armored divisions, were poised on the west bank of the Rhine. On March 7, an advance unit of the Ninth Armored Division discovered an intact railway bridge over the river at Remagen, and by evening, elements of three divisions had crossed the Ludendorff bridge. On March 23, Patton sent a division over the river by boat in the first amphibious crossing of the Rhine since Napoleon. At a press conference in Paris on March 27, Eisenhower called the Germans a whipped army, and the next day he informed Montgomery that taking Berlin was not an American priority. That afternoon, Marshall sent Ike a cable urging him to coordinate a linkup with the Russians, who were driving westward.

Throughout the war, Marshall had taken an ever-increasing role in global politics. After Yalta, President Roosevelt was exhausted. He was, in fact, dying, and, of necessity, even greater political responsibility fell to Marshall. This included the question of taking Berlin. Marshall minimized the political aspects of this objective, so long the focus of the Allies' advance through Europe. Instead, he allowed the supreme commander to view it strictly as a military goal. As such, in Eisenhower's view, it accounted for surprisingly little. When Ike asked Bradley what it might cost to take Berlin, Bradley estimated 100,000 casualties. Noting that the Yalta agreement would put the city in the Soviet zone,

General Bradley added, "A pretty stiff price for a prestige objective, especially when we've got to fall back and let the other fellow take over."[6]

Marshall agreed with Eisenhower that the greater military threat now lay to the south, in Bavaria, where it was believed that a "Nazi redoubt"—a concentration of diehard Nazi loyalists—planned to conduct a guerrilla war even after the capitulation of the German government. Consequently, on March 29, without conferring with the British, Eisenhower sent a message to Joseph Stalin saying that he was concentrating his forces on the south of Germany and not on taking Berlin. Stalin cabled back, "Your plans completely coincide with the plans of the Red Army. Berlin has lost its former strategic importance."

Of course, this would not stop Stalin from taking the prize himself.

For his part, Churchill was furious and cabled Eisenhower: "I deem it highly important that we should shake hands with the Russians as far east as possible." While Churchill objected through official channels that Ike had chosen not to reinforce Montgomery with American troops for a drive to Berlin ahead of the Russians, but instead had put the British troops in a secondary role well to the north of the city, the British press protested that their venerated war hero and the people of Britain had been relegated to a back seat just when victory was in sight.

Ike found himself on the receiving end of a series of telegrams, beginning with one from Marshall on March 29, questioning his message to "the Generalissimo," a reference to Churchill. Ike fired back, "Frankly the charge that I have changed plans has no possible basis in fact." He believed that Churchill knew full well that, regardless of how far east the U.S. forces drove in Germany, Churchill and Roosevelt had already agreed at Yalta that the American and British occupation zones would be limited on the east by a line two hundred miles *west* of Berlin.[7] In any case, Churchill threw in the towel, cabling Roosevelt at the "Little White House" in Warm Springs, Georgia, on April 6, "I regard the matter [of Berlin] as closed." He ended the message with "Amantium irae amoris integratio est," a Latin quotation that FDR's Map Room staff translated as, "Lovers' quarrels always go with true love."[8]

+>==+

On April 12, 1945, Eisenhower arrived in a B–25 bomber at a former Luftwaffe airbase near Wiesbaden, Germany, to join Bradley for a visit to Patton's headquarters at Hersfield. Patton had urged them to inspect a liberated Nazi concentration camp at Ohrdruf. "You'll never believe how bastardly these Krauts can be," he had told Bradley, "until you've seen this pesthole yourself."

"The things I saw beggar description," a shaken Eisenhower wrote to Marshall later that day. Recording that he and Patton had been sickened by the atrocities, he continued, "I made the visit deliberately, in order to be in a position to give firsthand evidence of these things if ever, in the future, there develops a tendency to charge these allegations merely to 'propaganda.'"

After a short flight to the village of Merkers, Patton took Eisenhower and Bradley to a 2,100-foot-deep salt mine in which the Germans had stored $100 billion worth of gold bullion, two million dollars in U.S. currency, and millions more in British, French, and Norwegian money. In another cave were hundreds of crates and boxes containing art treasures the Nazis had looted from all over Europe. That evening, the three generals who had smashed the German army in France sat in Patton's quarters close to where the Frankfurt autobahn forked toward Hanover and Dresden, each of which had been bombed into rubble. As Patton poured Ike a drink, the supreme commander was still pale from the visit to the death camp. Shaking his head, Eisenhower said, "I can't understand the mentality that would compel these German people to do a thing like that."

The generals went to bed around midnight, with Ike and Bradley in adjoining rooms of the former house of a German general, and Patton in his trailer, parked nearby. As Bradley was getting into bed, Patton knocked on the door and walked in. He had been listening to the BBC to get the time because his watch had stopped, he explained, when a voice broke into music and announced that President Roosevelt was dead.[9]

Late in the morning on Thursday, April 12, in Washington, D.C., Marshall left his office in the Pentagon early to go home for lunch with Katherine. As he was seated on the porch of Quarters No. 1 at Fort Myer after the meal, his aide, Colonel Frank McCarthy, arrived to break the news that the commander in chief was dead. McCarthy had learned of his death only because Mrs. Roosevelt had sent a message to the Pentagon for transmittal to Roosevelt's four sons, serving in uniform, saying that he had died and "would expect you to carry on and finish your jobs." Marshall rushed to the White House to offer his condolences and assistance. Mrs. Roosevelt asked him to assume the responsibility for all the details of bringing the president's body from Warm Springs, arranging a funeral service at the White House, and interment at Roosevelt's home at Hyde Park, New York.

On April 13, Marshall, the Navy and Air Force chiefs of staff, Stimson, and Secretary of the Navy James V. Forrestal met with the new president, Harry S. Truman. He had little to say to them, except that he was satisfied with the way the war was going and that he wanted them to continue as before. Riding back to the Pentagon with Secretary of War Stimson, Marshall deliberately withheld his opinion of Truman. Throughout his career, Marshall had made it his business to evaluate men on the basis of performance and results. Turning to Stimson, he said only of the new president, "We shall not know what he is really like until the pressure really begins."[10]

One week later, as the Red Army swarmed into Berlin, Hitler killed himself in his bunker deep beneath the shell-shattered Reich chancellery. Five days after his burned corpse was discovered in a shallow hole in what had been a garden, patrols of the U.S. Sixty-ninth Infantry and Russian Fifty-eighth Guards Divisions met at the Elbe River, which now divided Germany between the U.S.-dominated West and the Soviet-dominated East. On May 6, the German chief of staff, General Alfred Jodl, arrived at a schoolhouse in Reims that served as Eisenhower's headquarters to talk of ending the war. The U.S. terms were "unconditional surrender," and Jodl capitulated the next day.

Ike cabled Marshall: "The mission of this Allied Force was fulfilled at 0241, local time, May 7, 1945."

Marshall replied: "You have made history, great history for the good of mankind and you have stood for all we hope for and admire in an officer of the United States Army. These are my tributes and personal thanks."

In a letter to Marshall dated May 8, 1945, Eisenhower more than returned the compliment: "Our army and our people have never been so deeply indebted to any other soldier."[11]

CHAPTER 15

War and Peace

THE EXCHANGE OF LAURELS FOLLOWING THE GERMAN SURRENDER
felt good, but Marshall knew the war was only half over at best. Even before
Jodl's capitulation, the chief of staff had been juggling manpower, beginning
the transfer of America's armies to the Pacific. He presided over a point-based
rotation system in which soldiers with the highest number of points (based
on length and nature of service) would be sent home, would march in any
number of victory parades, and then—most of them—be discharged. About
1.8 million men fell into this category. The rest of the U.S. Army currently
serving in Europe or earmarked for service there, some six million, would be
diverted to the war against Japan. Marshall contemplated a rapid transfer of
soldiers and gear that dwarfed the initial mobilization for the European war
and made his spectacular management of the transfer of the St. Mihiel com-
batants to the Meuse-Argonne campaign in World War I seem modest by
comparison.

There was no question but that Japan had already lost the war. The
hellish fact was, however, that in defeat, Japan was taking an *escalating* toll

on American forces. Marshall was so desperate to bring the war to an end that he ordered his Operations Division to study the use of disabling gases—chemical weapons intended to wreak less than lethal havoc—in all the campaigns approaching the Japanese home islands themselves. His objective was to drive Japanese defensive garrisons out of their tunnels and bunkers. Marshall proposed that once the invasion of the home islands was under way, widespread use of disabling gases would force soldiers as well as civilians to wear gas masks at all times, a situation that (as he knew from World War I) created general demoralization and physical debilitation. Weakened mentally and physically, the enemy would be more vulnerable to conquest.

In the end, British objections—the most vehement of them voiced by Winston Churchill—forced Marshall to abandon any thought of chemical warfare. The irony was that, after the atomic bomb had been successfully tested in the New Mexico desert on July 16, 1945, Churchill had no objection to using this far deadlier weapon fraught with far graver moral consequences. But before "the bomb" was shown to be a viable weapon, Marshall oversaw the final planning stages of Operation Olympic, an assault on Kyushu, southernmost of the Japanese home islands, and Operation Coronet, the invasion of Honshu, Japan's main island.

As if the overwhelming strategic and logistical challenges of these mammoth invasions—both many times larger than the D-Day invasion of Normandy had been—were not burden enough, Marshall had to contend with a pair of massive military egos. Before he died, President Roosevelt had designated Douglas MacArthur over Admiral Chester A. Nimitz to lead Operation Coronet. To say that this made Chief of Naval Operations Admiral Ernest J. King unhappy would be an extreme understatement. (Since March 1942 King had been not only chief of naval operations but also commander in chief of the U.S. Fleet.) King insisted to Marshall that, even if MacArthur were put in charge of Coronet, command of the fleet itself had to remain in navy hands. In response, Marshall formulated a new version of the unified command concept—not one that aimed to eliminate distinctions of nationality, but of service branch. He declared in a memorandum to King that "Control of the naval resources directly involved in putting armies ashore is essential to the success of the operation and must be given to the commander having primary responsibility for the operation."[1]

Marshall had articulated what would become the cornerstone principle of the modern "integrated arms" approach to warfighting, in which the personnel and equipment of all service branches, air, ground, and sea, are not only put under a single commander, but are subject to fully integrated planning. Most immediately, the effects of this doctrine would be seen in the creation of a cabinet-level Department of Defense with the National Security Act of 1947, which replaced the Department of War (primarily concerned with the army) and assumed jurisdiction over all service branches, including the U.S. Air Force, which the act established independently from the U.S. Army. The trend toward integration, however, has continued beyond the level of administration and now governs virtually all military planning and every major operation. Nevertheless, in 1945, King continued to resist Marshall's direction, not only refusing to acknowledge MacArthur as overall commander of Operation Coronet, but even declining to designate *any* overall commander. An exasperated and alarmed Marshall realized that he had to give King a way to comply that would save his face as well as that of the navy. The chief of staff affirmed FDR's choice of MacArthur as Coronet commander, but specified that MacArthur would issue orders to the navy only in case of exigency and only then through the operation's naval commander. The point was that MacArthur would still call the shots, but would do so with restraint and via the naval chain of command. King agreed.

George Marshall had known about the existence of the Manhattan Project and its work toward the creation of an atomic bomb long before Truman was fully briefed by Secretary of War Henry Stimson some two weeks after he became president. Although Marshall had been unfazed by the prospect of employing chemical weapons against the Japanese, he was profoundly ambivalent about the atomic bomb. In contrast to Dwight Eisenhower, who did not believe the weapon should be used under any circumstance, Marshall ultimately favored its use strictly on military grounds as a means of shortening the war and thereby saving American (and even Japanese) lives. A participant in the meetings of the so-called Interim Committee, which President Truman had created to advise him on nuclear weapons, Marshall advocated dropping the first bomb on a strictly military target, such as a naval installation, to demonstrate its lethality. Like some others, including a number of Manhattan Project scientists, he also suggested giving serious consideration to staging some sort of demonstration of the lethality of the bomb for Japanese government and military representatives, perhaps by detonating it on some uninhabited Pacific island. Both of these proposals were overruled by James F. Byrnes, Truman's personal representative at the committee's meetings (who replaced Edward Stettinius as secretary of state in July). In the end, Marshall concurred with President Truman's decision to use atomic weapons directly against Japanese cities of military importance—though he was relieved that the decision was Truman's and not his to make.

Truman and Marshall received word of the success of the July 16 atomic bomb test while they were in the Berlin suburb of Potsdam hammering out the political shape of the postwar world with Churchill, Stalin, and their respective military and civilian advisers. While the leaders wrangled with one another, they were all agreed on one thing: George Marshall was a "great man." That was the phrase Truman would use to describe him lifelong. Churchill, at Potsdam, pronounced him "the noblest Roman of them all" and praised his ability to persuade the U.S. Congress into doing the right thing while also ensuring that America's soldiers arrived in theater highly trained. As for Stalin, he pointed to Marshall as they sat at table together during a dinner hosted by the British Potsdam delegation and proclaimed, "That is a man I admire. He is a good general," then, curiously, continued: "We have good generals in the Soviet Army . . . . Only ours still lack breeding, and their manners are bad."[2] Marshall did not, however, admire Stalin, and the one thing that he welcomed without ambivalence about the successful test of the atomic bomb was that it would very likely render unnecessary any Soviet participation in the planned, potential invasion of Japan. Marshall was under no illusions concerning Stalin's territorial designs.

It took two atomic bombings, against Hiroshima on August 6, 1945, and Nagasaki three days later, to bring about Japan's surrender, which was formally received aboard the battleship USS *Missouri* riding at anchor in Tokyo Bay on September 2. George C. Marshall imagined that the surrender heralded his retirement, to which, after thirty-eight years in uniform, he looked forward.

Since his graduation from VMI, he had been awarded the Distinguished Service Medal, Silver Star, Victory Medal, and German Occupation Medal for World War I; the Philippine Campaign Medal; three World War II theater ribbons, the National Defense Ribbon, and decorations from seventeen foreign countries. On November 26, 1945, President Truman added an Oak Leaf Cluster to his Distinguished Service Medal. The accompanying citation began, "In a war unparalleled in magnitude and in horror, millions of Americans gave their country outstanding service. General of the Army George C. Marshall gave it victory." The concluding paragraph read:

Statesmen and Soldier, he had courage, fortitude, and vision, and best of all a rare self-effacement. He has been a tower of strength to two Commanders in Chief. His standards of character, conduct and efficiency inspired the entire Army, the Nation and the world. To him, as much as to any individual, the United States owes its future. He takes his place at the head of the great commanders of history.

Relieved as chief of staff on November 30, 1945, at his own request, George Marshall was succeeded by Dwight Eisenhower. Katherine Marshall looked forward to her husband's retirement even more than he did, and she was appalled when the call came from President Truman asking the general to undertake a mission to China, bearing the personal rank of ambassador, for the purpose of negotiating a truce in the struggle between the Nationalist government of Chiang Kai-shek and Mao Zedong's communists. As Churchill and Truman had feared (and Roosevelt less so), the end of World War II invited a global dissemination of communism. Truman's policy with regard to China was to prevent this giant from entering the Soviet sphere by forging a coalition government between the pro-Western, capitalistic Chiang and (from the U.S. point of view) the pro-Soviet communist Mao. The inducement would come in the form of half a billion U.S. dollars in aid.

Marshall arrived in China on December 20, 1945, and wasted no time in bringing the two sides together. Once together, however, they spent most of the next two years in fruitless discussion—or, rather, they exploited the truce time to better prepare to fight one another. In May 1946, Eisenhower arrived at Marshall's home in Nanking. It was Ike's first trip to the Far East to assess U.S. troop readiness, but he bore a request from President Truman that Marshall consider returning to the United States to replace the ailing James Byrnes as secretary of state.

"Great goodness, Eisenhower," exclaimed Marshall. "I would take any job in the world to get out of this one. I'd even enlist in the Army."[3]

He made one request, however, that he be permitted to remain in China until September in the hope of working out a permanent truce. He stayed even longer, as his efforts to reconcile Chiang and Mao dragged on until January 1947.

"I tried to please everyone," Marshall said. "The result was that by the time I left, nobody trusted me."

With the collapse of the "Marshall Mission," as it was being called, the Chinese Civil War, which had begun in 1927 and was suspended during World War II, resumed, and by 1949, Chiang Kai-shek's Nationalists had been defeated, and Mao established the People's Republic of China. The biggest nation on the planet had "gone communist." Marshall believed he knew where the blame lay. If Chiang Kai-shek had not been immersed in corruption and had cared about and attended to the woeful plight of the Chinese people, Marshall said, he could have "knocked the props out from under Mao."[4]

Unanimously confirmed as secretary of state by the Republican-controlled Senate (the 1946 midterm elections gave the GOP control of both houses of Congress), Marshall arrived at the State Department on January 27, 1947. Although he dressed in civilian clothes, the diplomats and civil servants learned that he expected to be addressed not as "Mr. Secretary," but by his military rank. "This was not because General Marshall had a trace of arrogance or stiffness popularly attributed to high military personages," noted Undersecretary of State Dean Acheson. "Rationing his none-too-ebullient energy to meet great demands laid upon it led to an aloofness, an ungregariousness, which was not ungraciousness."[5]

Less than a month after taking charge of the State Department, the general who had spent much of his time as army chief of staff resisting Winston Churchill's pleas for an Allied drive into the Mediterranean region and then into the Balkans—largely to prevent their postwar domination by the Soviet Union—was presented with his first international crisis. While he was appearing at Columbia University on February 21, 1947, to accept an honorary degree, he was informed that Britain had decided it could no longer bear the costs of providing military and other aid to prop up the government of Greece against a takeover by a Moscow-backed Communist insurgency. Both Marshall and the president understood that if Greece fell, Turkey would follow, giving the Soviet Union mastery over the entire eastern Mediterranean. Determined to find a way to prevent this, Truman convened a meeting with congressional leaders at the White House on February 27 to lay out a plan for U.S. aid to Greece and Turkey.

"It is not alarmist to say," Marshall asserted at the meeting, "that we are faced with the first crisis of a series which might extend Soviet domination to Europe, the Middle East and Asia." Dean Acheson later wrote of the crisis, "I knew we were met at Armageddon . . . . The Soviet Union was playing one of the greatest gambles in history. . . . We and we alone were in a position to break up the play."[6]

On March 12, 1947, Truman asked a joint session of Congress to authorize financial aid to Greece and Turkey. He told the legislators that it must be the policy of the United States to support free peoples who were resisting attempted subjugation from within or outside pressures. This declaration became known as "the Truman Doctrine" and marked the start of a U.S policy of the "containment of Communism" that would last throughout the long Cold War.

The question for the United States in the spring 1947 was whether the war-ravaged and struggling nations of Western Europe would be able to join the United States in thwarting the Soviet aim of communizing the continent. In his first speech as secretary of state, Marshall told a group of businessmen at Princeton University, "If the world is to get on its feet, if the productive facilities of the world are to be restored, if democratic processes in many countries are to resume their functioning, a strong and definite assistance from the United States will be necessary." In a later radio address, he spoke of "impoverished and suffering people of Europe who are crying for help."[7]

The Potsdam Conference (1945) had come and gone without producing any specific plan for European recovery and reconstruction. The U.S.

Congress voted U.S. financial aid, but 1945 and, even more, 1946, with its especially brutal winter, nevertheless brought great hardship to Germany and the rest of Europe. Like Truman, Marshall believed that former treasury secretary Henry Morgenthau Jr. had been very wrong to propose at the 1944 Bretton Woods conference a postwar economic policy (the so-called Morgenthau Plan) to punish Germany by reducing it to a kind of subsistence agricultural state. This, both Truman and Marshall believed, would repeat the errors of the Versailles peace agreement that followed World War I, creating the bitter political and economic climate conducive to the rise of another Hitler or, even more likely, to a Soviet-controlled communist takeover of all Germany.

Marshall took the insight event further than Truman. He understood that many Americans felt the way Morgenthau had: that it was wrong to aid the recovery of Germany, a nation that had twice plunged the world into catastrophic war. But, Marshall pointed out, Germany had been the most powerful industrial and economic force in Europe between the two world wars. As long as Germany lay prostrate, the economy of all Europe would remain in a postwar depression. Wanting vengeance on Germany was understandable, but if Europe was to recover and stay out of Soviet communist hands, some way had to be found to compel the political leaders and people of Europe to act cooperatively.

Like everyone else in the Truman administration, Marshall had read the analysis of Soviet postwar expansion that U.S. diplomat George F. Kennan had published in the July 1947 issue of *Foreign Affairs*. Marshall agreed with Kennan's recommendations for "containing" the spread of communism, and he supported the so-called Truman Doctrine, the president's policy of using economic and, if necessary, military measures to contain Soviet aggression. Although he had been the senior general of the U.S. Army, Marshall wanted to ensure that economic, not military, means took precedence in executing the Truman Doctrine. He therefore concluded that a massive U.S.-financed plan of aid would best serve the strategic purpose of containment. Indeed, Marshall entertained the hope that Stalin could be persuaded to cooperate with the plan. This hope was shattered at the Foreign Ministers' Conference held in Moscow from March 10 to April 24, 1947, organized ostensibly to formulate a plan for European recovery. Marshall, who had endured nearly two years of frustration during his Chinese mission, immediately recognized that the last thing the Soviets wanted was European recovery. Their intention was to thwart and stall reconstruction. Stalin understood that the worse off a region was, the riper it was for gathering into the Soviet sphere.

Marshall assigned Kennan and another State Department diplomat, William L. Clayton, to outline a plan for European recovery under U.S. sponsorship. The problem Marshall needed Kennan and Clayton to solve was how to create an *American*-funded plan that *European* states would freely accept. At all costs, any whiff of Yankee imperialism—a problem that had plagued U.S. foreign policy since the Spanish-American War of 1898 and would repeatedly resurface throughout the twentieth century and into the twenty-first—had to be avoided. This prompted Marshall to specify the creation of a plan that would be funded exclusively by the United States, but would be entirely administered by Europe.

It was a solution as bold as it was brilliant. Such a plan would serve the urgent need for humanitarian relief—people were starving—and, because it would be self-administered, it would force the nations of Europe to unite in cooperation. Marshall specified to Kennan and Clayton that the plan's funds had to be made conditional upon all participants' agreeing on a single, unitary plan of distribution and use. No money would be released until such a plan had been created and approved.

Once Kennan and Clayton had completed the outline of the European recovery plan, Marshall had to secure approval of it from both the American public and the U.S. Congress. He persuaded President Truman that the best approach was to spring the plan suddenly, present it as a fait accompli in order to avoid protracted debate. On June 5, 1947, in a commencement speech at Harvard University, Marshall presented the plan in its barest bones, disavowing any political or ideological purpose, but calling on the leaders of Europe to convene to create their own plan for European recovery, which the United States would fund. No dollar amounts were specified, and Marshall had colluded with President Truman to minimize press coverage of the speech. It was not announced to reporters or journalists; indeed, the president purposely scheduled a White House press conference on other matters on the very day of the Harvard address. Meanwhile, Marshall instructed Undersecretary of State Dean Acheson to contact every *European* news organization to ensure that coverage of the proposal would sweep Europe. Marshall's objective was to make a pledge to the European people so public that no

American politician, no matter how conservative, would want to appear to break an American promise.

The stratagem worked, and all of Europe buzzed. Now Marshall swung into action, touring the United States in the equivalent of a full-out political campaign to bring the plan directly to the American people. Such was the wide respect Marshall enjoyed among most of the American public that a majority of the people eagerly embraced it. Truman agreed that the plan's official title, the "European Recovery Plan," lacked popular appeal, but when his young aide Clark Clifford proposed calling it the "Truman Plan," the president exploded. Telling Clifford that this was the surest way to kill it in the Republican Congress, Truman decreed that it would be dubbed the "Marshall Plan."

Into the early spring of 1948, Congress debated the Marshall Plan, which passed the Senate on March 14 and the House on March 31.

As implemented, the Marshall Plan became perhaps the most spectacularly successful foreign policy program any world power has ever produced. It was America's most powerful "weapon" in the Cold War, a humanitarian, economic, and political triumph. George Catlett Marshall, an architect of American and Allied victory in World War II, would be remembered even more as the architect of the plan that bears his name.

Yet no sooner was the Marshall Plan voted into reality and set into motion than, on June 19, 1948, the city of Berlin that he and General Dwight D. Eisenhower had decided in April 1945 was not worth the cost in American G.I. lives to capture, suddenly became a flashpoint of a potential *third* world war and Marshall's most dangerous crisis as secretary of state.

Reacting to an announcement by the United States, Britain, and France that they intended to meld their zones of occupation in Germany into the separate democratic state of West Germany, the Soviets shut off all land access to the U.S., British, and French zones in Berlin, deep within the Soviet zone of Germany. Truman, Marshall, others in the administration, and the leaders of the U.S. military convened to formulate a response to the Berlin blockade. Ever the realist, Marshall held that the rapidly demobilized U.S. Army in Germany lacked the power to force open the routes. If they tried, they would be overwhelmed, and the United States would have no choice but to make a massive retaliation against the Soviet Union itself. With U.S. conventional forces depleted by postwar demobilization, retaliation would almost certainly involve the use of whatever atomic weapons lay in American stockpiles. The resulting war would further devastate an already war-torn Europe. Marshall agreed with the president that, instead of taking aggressive action on the ground, the least dangerous response was to supply the Western Zones of Berlin by a massive airlift. He then summoned the Soviet ambassador in Washington to a meeting and warned him that the United States would not be induced by threats, pressures, or other Soviet actions to abandon its rights to free access to Berlin.

The Berlin Airlift was a triumph for the brand-new U.S. Air Force, whose planes (along with those of the British RAF) carried coal and food into West Berlin's Templehof Airport around the clock for nearly a year, sometimes at the rate of one landing every two minutes. During this time, President Truman was locked in a tight election contest with Thomas E. Dewey, the Republican almost universally favored to defeat the incumbent. The campaign was bitter, and Truman directed it as much against what he called the "worst-ever," "do-nothing" Republican-controlled Eightieth Congress as he did against Dewey. Against the predictions of the pundits, Truman would defeat Dewey, but the divide between Republicans and Democrats would produce vicious attacks against the president and virtually everyone in his administration, including George Marshall.

While Truman campaigned, an exhausted Marshall entered Walter Reed Army Hospital in Washington for a complete physical. He had been suffering severe abdominal and back pains, and was diagnosed with an enlarged right kidney, which required surgical removal. Faced with the ongoing Berlin crisis and negotiations that resulted from it to create with former World War II allies a North Atlantic mutual defense pact—the North Atlantic Treaty Organization (NATO)—as well as the November meeting of the United Nations General Assembly in New York, Marshall put off the surgery until December.

The postponement took an added toll on his health. Marshall told the president that he would remain in his post until the inauguration in January of the winner of the election, which had yet to take place, but that he would then retire. The surgery, which was performed on December 7, 1948, was successful, and, true to his word, Marshall served through to the end of Truman's first term. Retiring on January 20, 1949, he was succeeded as secretary of state by Dean Acheson.

With Katherine, Marshall settled into their home in Leesburg, Virginia. He accepted undemanding positions on the board of directors of Pan American Airlines, as a trustee of the American Institute of Pacific Relations, and as a member of the American Battle Monuments Commission. He eagerly accepted an invitation on April 4, 1949, to attend the ceremonial signing of the pact creating the North Atlantic Treaty Organization, which was the most immediate outgrowth of the Berlin crisis. Although he also accepted President Truman's request that he assume leadership of the American Red Cross, calling it "too great an opportunity and challenge to be ignored," Marshall had every reason to assume that his career in public service and his role in history were at a well-deserved and honorable end.

CHAPTER 16

Soldier Statesman

GEORGE MARSHALL ASSUMED HIS POST AT THE AMERICAN RED CROSS on September 22, 1949. Less than a year later, while he was fishing at a resort in Huron Mountain, Michigan, he received a call from the White House. The president told him that he had something to discuss in person when he returned from vacation. Marshall agreed, and, on September 6, 1950, Harry Truman asked him to become the nation's third Secretary of Defense. The logistical and political complexities attendant on the creation of the Department of Defense in 1947 had almost certainly contributed to the mental breakdown and subsequent suicide of the first secretary, James V. Forrestal, in 1949. Now the second secretary, Louis A. Johnson, was about to resign, having lost Truman's confidence and having absorbed the blame from Republicans for what was regarded as the faltering conduct of the Korean War. For anyone, the prospect of becoming the third secretary would have loomed as formidable. For a man in the twilight of a long and exhausting career, in delicate health, it boded little good.

At the direction of both Congress and President Truman, Louis A. Johnson and Forrestal before him had presided over the precipitous reduction of the U.S. military and therefore Johnson had little to work with when Communist North Korean troops surged across the 38th parallel into the Republic of Korea (South Korea) on June 25, 1950. (The 38th parallel was a line of demarcation established at the Potsdam Conference in July 1945; north of this latitude the USSR would accept the surrender of Japanese forces in Korea, and below it the United States would accept Japan's surrender. The line endured as the border between North and South Korea.) Truman put Douglas MacArthur in command of the U.S.-dominated United Nations forces whose mission was to defend South Korea, but when MacArthur advocated expanding the war and wrote a letter to the Veterans of Foreign Wars criticizing Truman's policy of fighting a limited war rather than committing to what MacArthur called "victory," Truman put Johnson in the impossible position of reining MacArthur in. This led to a breach between Johnson and the president, who then forced Johnson's resignation. Thus Marshall was being invited into a hornet's nest. He was to preside over a Department of Defense in disarray, with a military so reduced as to be inadequate to effectively meet the threat in this new war with the forces of communism, and having to contend with a president and theater commander who were at each other's throats.

Despite all the reasons to turn down the job, Marshall replied to the president that he had "only to tell me what you want, and I'll do it." As the architect and champion of unified command in World War II, Marshall had been a driving force behind the creation of the Department of Defense as the ultimate means of achieving and institutionalizing unity of America's military. He wanted to ensure that the department would succeed. Certainly, he did not want to see it shattered on the rocks of the conflict in Korea, nor did he want to see that conflict escalate into a third world war. Yet he continued in his response to the president: "But I want you to think about the fact that my appointment may reflect upon you and your administration." What he meant by this was that the Republican right wing, now led by the likes of red-baiting Wisconsin senator Joseph McCarthy, blamed him for the "loss" of China to communism. "I want to help, not hurt you," Marshall told the president. For his part, Truman was overwhelmed by the character of the man. "Can you think of anyone else saying that?" he wrote to his wife, Bess. "I can't, and he's one of the *great*."[1]

Truman nominated Marshall as secretary of defense, bringing down upon the president just what Marshall had feared it would: a firestorm of protest from Republicans, led by McCarthy and his ally Senator William Jenner of Indiana, who, predictably, accused Truman's administration of being "soft on Communism," and Marshall of having undercut Chiang Kai-shek's Nationalist government, resulting in the victory of Mao Zedong's Communists in 1949. Jenner went even further, taking to the Senate floor to accuse Marshall of being "a living lie" and a "front man" for "traitors." In moment of high drama not seen in the Senate since perhaps the days leading up to the Civil War, Massachusetts Senator Leverett Saltonstall—a Republican—leapt to his feet to exclaim that "if ever there was a life spent in the interest of our country, a life that is not a lie, it is the life of George C. Marshall."[2] Five days later, the Senate confirmed Marshall's nomination by a vote of 57 to eleven. Sworn in on September 21, 1950, Marshall became the only former general to have served both as secretary of state and secretary of defense.

As head of all the U.S. armed services, Marshall found himself once more working with Eisenhower, whom Truman had tapped with the assent of the European members of NATO to command the defense alliance; with Omar Bradley, who was now chairman of the U.S. Joint Chiefs of Staff, another manifestation of unified command; J. Lawton "Lightning Joe" Collins, U.S. Army Chief of Staff; and Douglas MacArthur, once more in command of Americans at war in the Far East.

Thanks to MacArthur's daring amphibious assault at Inchon on September 15, 1950, North Korean forces were quickly pushed back beyond the 38th parallel; however, in November, a massive influx of Communist Chinese forces pushed the U.S.–UN troops back into South Korea. By early 1951, the Eighth U.S. Army under Matthew Ridgway stabilized UN lines along the 37th parallel. By this time, the United Nations had voted on a resolution to end the war, and the Truman administration and other Allied leaders decided to abandon as a war aim the reunification of the Korean nation under democratic rule and instead to settle for driving the communist invaders out of South Korea and reaching an armistice based on the division of the Korean peninsula at the 38th parallel. General MacArthur protested this policy and, once again, proclaimed that there was no substitute for victory. In April 1951, he sent a letter to right-wing Republican Speaker of the House Joseph W. Martin, disagreeing with Truman's policy of limiting the war to avoid a larger war with China; Martin read the letter into the *Congressional Record,* thereby making it public. Also, without authorization, MacArthur sent an ultimatum to the Communist Chinese forces, which wrecked Truman's efforts to negotiate a cease-fire.

On April 6, the day after Speaker Martin made MacArthur's letter public, President Truman summoned Marshall, W. Averell Harriman (who had been an adviser to FDR throughout World War II), Secretary of State Dean Acheson, and Joint Chiefs Chairman Omar Bradley to ask their advice on what to do with MacArthur. Harriman said MacArthur should have been fired two years earlier. Marshall was concerned about the possible political repercussions that might follow the dismissal of MacArthur. He advised caution in firing a hero of two world wars who was popular with the general public and with Republicans, who had eyes on the 1952 elections as well as the power in Congress to affect military appropriations. Acheson believed MacArthur should be relieved, but only after a unanimous decision to do so by the Joint Chiefs of Staff. Bradley said MacArthur had acted in an insubordinate manner and he deserved to be fired, but he told Truman he wished to talk with General Collins before making a final recommendation.

Truman asked all of his advisers to return the next day for more discussion, and directed Marshall to restudy all messages exchanged with MacArthur in the past two years. The next morning, the group met again in Truman's office. Marshall told the president that after reading all the messages he agreed that MacArthur should have been relieved two years earlier because of repeated violations of the constitutional chain of command. Before the brief meeting ended, Truman directed Bradley to obtain the views of the remaining Joint Chiefs of Staff and to be prepared to make a final recommendation on April 9.

Bradley, Collins, General Hoyt Vandenberg, and others met on the afternoon of April 8 in the Pentagon to discuss military aspects of MacArthur's relief. At the end of this meeting, they conferred briefly with Marshall. All of the Joint Chiefs of Staff agreed that from the military viewpoint the relief of MacArthur should be carried out. There was no formal vote, but their unanimous view was that MacArthur had been insubordinate.

On April 9, Truman made the decision to relieve General MacArthur of his command in the Far East. By presidential order, MacArthur on his return to the United States was to receive full military honors, and Truman gave government employees the day off—which added to the crowd lining the way to the Capitol, where both houses of Congress waited in joint session to hear an address that Speaker Martin had invited MacArthur to give. In answer to those who had said he wanted a wider war, MacArthur told the assembled legislators that he knew war as few other men living knew it, and nothing to him was more revolting. In deep and rolling tones, he said that once war was forced upon the nation, there was no alternative but to apply every means to win it. War's very object, he said, was victory.

Carried coast-to-coast on television to an audience of unprecedented size, MacArthur's dramatic speech gave credibility to charges by Senator McCarthy and other Republicans in Congress that the Truman administration was crawling with officials who were either outright traitors working on behalf of the Soviet Union or unwitting accomplices in a campaign of Communist subversion. In a long and rambling speech—the manuscript ran to 169 pages—delivered on the Senate floor on June 14, 1951, McCarthy charged Marshall with shaping a carefully planned retreat from victory in Korea. He said that Marshall had fostered policies favorable to the Soviets throughout World War II, which included handing the Russians Berlin, and that, after the war, he had engineered the loss of China to the Communists. McCarthy did not apply the words *treason* or *traitor* to Marshall, but he did put him at the head of a "conspiracy . . . to diminish the United States in world affairs" and to weaken the nation militarily to "the end that we shall be contained, frustrated and finally fall victim to Soviet intrigue from within and Russian military might from without." McCarthy worked himself up to a literally Shakespearian peroration, comparing Marshall to Macbeth, a man "stepped in [blood] so far" that he could not turn back, could not repent, could not correct his course.[3]

Marshall, assailed by reporters, refused to defend himself, explaining to Clayton Fritchey, a popular columnist, that "if I have to explain at this point that I am not a traitor to the United States, I hardly think it's worth it."[4]

Others rushed not so much to Marshall's defense—for they felt that Marshall's record of service spoke for itself—as they did to condemn what Adlai E. Stevenson, at the time governor of Illinois and soon to be a Democratic candidate for president, aptly described as a "hysterical form of putrid slander."[5]

History identifies the televised Army-McCarthy hearings of 1954 as the event that precipitated the fall of Joseph McCarthy, but it was his raving against Marshall that did more to polarize public opinion and begin to solidify the opposition that would eventually bring down the junior senator from Wisconsin. Nevertheless, the speech may have driven Marshall to resign on September 12, 1951, although the fact is that, at seventy, he was tired and had been contemplating resignation well before McCarthy's tirade.

He left without either military or civilian fanfare, returned to Leesburg, and declined President Truman's offer to reappoint him to the presidency of the Red Cross, though he accepted, once again, a seat on the American Battle Monuments Commission. He also declined many invitations to receptions and dinners in Washington, making an exception for a small affair at the British Embassy honoring Winston Churchill in January 1952. In September of that year, he and Katherine sailed to Europe, where he inspected the U.S. military cemeteries. At Anzio, Katherine put flowers on her son's grave.

When they returned from Europe, the presidential election campaign was in full swing, with two men Marshall highly respected in contention. Dwight Eisenhower had won the Republican nomination and Democrats had chosen Adlai Stevenson, whom Marshall had asked to serve as an alternate to the U.S. United Nations delegation in 1947 and who had staunchly defended Marshall against McCarthy. Eisenhower, of course, owed his lofty World War II command to Marshall. Professionally, two men could not have been closer. Yet, Republicans so feared Senator McCarthy in 1952 that Eisenhower, in a speech he was to make in McCarthy's home state, gave in to campaign advisers who urged him to delete a direct rebuke of McCarthy's frequent attacks on Marshall. The deletion was discovered by a reporter for the *New York Times* and featured on the front page the next day. Eisenhower was widely criticized for abandoning his personal convictions, and Truman excoriated him for betraying his principles and for deserting a friend. Marshall said nothing publicly, but told his goddaughter, Rose Page Wilson, that Ike had been forced into a compromise. Only after he had won the election did an apparently repentant President Eisenhower make certain that Marshall and Katherine were invited to his inauguration and White House ceremonies for visiting heads of state, and in March 1953, shortly after his inauguration, Eisenhower named Marshall to head the American delegation at the coronation of Queen Elizabeth II. In a series of reunions with World War II colleagues in London, Marshall even spent a day at the races with Churchill.

He would return to Europe in December 1953. His destination this time was Oslo, Norway, where he was to receive the Nobel Peace Prize, having been nominated by former president Truman and others to honor his role in the creation and implementation of the Marshall Plan. It was a hard trip for him, since he was recovering from a month-long siege of the flu, but he undertook the journey and accepted the award, he explained to reporters, as "a tribute to the whole American people."[6] To this day, George Marshall remains the only soldier ever to receive the award. Joe McCarthy and those of his ilk dared not criticize the award, especially since the only dissenting voices came from the leaders of the Soviet bloc.

On his return to the United States, Marshall found himself assailed by the lingering effects of the flu, and he would never fully recover his health. Declining publishers' offers of lucrative contracts for his memoirs, he did agree to give Forrest C. Pogue, official U.S. Army historian of World War II, a series of interviews under the auspices of the recently formed George C. Marshall Research Foundation, which had been established on the VMI campus in Lexington, Virginia. Pogue conducted the interviews in 1956 and 1957, which resulted in a four-volume biography, the first three of which— *George C. Marshall: Education of a General, 1880–1939* (1963), *Ordeal and Hope, 1939–1943* (1966), and *Organizer of Victory* (1973), Marshall's early life and military career, and the last, *Statesman, 1945–1959* (1987), devoted to his postwar diplomatic career. Published to wide acclaim by Viking, the four volumes remain a monument to the man and the starting point for all research on Marshall.

On January 14, 1959, two weeks after his seventy-ninth birthday, Marshall suffered a crippling stroke, and on February 18, 1959, he was hit by another. Eisenhower visited him at Walter Reed Army Hospital three times, accompanied once by eighty-four-year-old Winston Churchill, who stood in the doorway, speechless and with tears in his eyes, gazing at his wartime comrade, now in coma. Marshall died shortly past 6:00 P.M. on Friday, October 16, 1959.

His body lay in repose in Bethlehem Chapel at the Washington National Cathedral for twenty-four hours, beginning at noon on October 19. The next day, the body was taken to the post chapel at Fort Myer, Virginia, for the funeral service, attended by a small number of invited guests. A private burial service was held at Arlington National Cemetery. George Catlett Marshall Jr. was laid to rest in Section 7, a little to the east of the Memorial Amphitheater, beside his first wife, Elizabeth Coles Marshall, and her mother. Marshall's request for a simple service was honored. His wartime aide and orderly, his current orderly, and other wartime friends and colleagues, including Walter Bedell Smith, Admiral Harold Stark, and Omar Bradley, followed his coffin, accompanied by Katherine Marshall (who would live many more years, until December 18, 1979), to a sloping Arlington National Cemetery plot just below the Tomb of the Unknown Soldier.

Notes

Introduction

1. *First Biennial Report on the State of the Armed Forces of the Chief of Staff of the U.S. Army.* Washington, D.C.: U.S. Army, 1941.
2. Cray, Ed. *General of the Army: George C. Marshall, Soldier and Statesman.* New York: W. W. Norton, 1990, p. 132.
3. Mosley, Leonard. *Hero for Our Times.* New York: Hearst Books, 1982, p. 122.
4. Ibid., p. 127.

Chapter 1

1. Bland, Larry I., ed. *George C. Marshall: Interviews and Reminiscences for Forrest C. Pogue.* Lexington, Va.: G. C. Marshall Research Foundation, 1991, p. 58.
2. Ibid.
3. Ibid., p. 38.
4. Ibid., p. 98.
5. Mosley, Leonard. *Marshall: Hero for Our Times,* New York: Hearst Books, 1982, p. 19.
6. Bland, ed., *George C. Marshall: Interviews and Reminiscences,* p. 144.
7. Ibid., p. 141.
8. Mosley, *Marshall,* p. 23.

Chapter 2

1. Bland, Larry I., ed. *George C. Marshall: Interviews and Reminiscences for Forrest C. Pogue.* Lexington, Va.: G. C. Marshall Research Foundation, 1991, p. 147.
2. Cray, Ed. *General of the Army: George C. Marshall, Soldier and Statesman.* New York: W. W. Norton, 1990, p. 134.
3. Ibid., p. 36.
4. Manchester, William. *American Caesar: Douglas MacArthur, 1880–1964.* Boston: Little, Brown, 1978, p. 171.
5. Arnold, Henry H. *Global Mission.* New York: Harper, 1949, p. 44
6. Ibid.

7. Pogue, Forrest C. *George Marshall.* Vol. 1. *Education of a General, 1880–1939.* New York: Viking, 1963, p. 124.

8. General E. W. Nichols to Marshall, November 22, 1919. VMI files.

Chapter 3

1. Efficiency report signed by Lieutenant Colonel Johnson Hagood, December 11, 1916, and quoted in Cray, Ed. *General of the Army: George C. Marshall, Soldier and Statesman.* New York: W. W. Norton, 1990, p. 47.

2. Marshall, George C. *Memoirs of My Services in the World War, 1917–1918.* Foreword and notes by James L. Collins Jr. Boston: Houghton Mifflin, 1976, p. 6.

3. Ibid., p. 19.

4. Ibid., p. 18.

5. Bland, Larry I., ed. *George C. Marshall: Interviews and Reminiscences for Forrest C. Pogue.* Lexington, Va.: G. C. Marshall Research Foundation, 1991, pp. 196 – 198.

6. Ibid., p. 211.

7. Marshall, *Memoirs of My Services in the World War, 1917–1918,* p. 79.

8. Ibid., pp. 94–97.

Chapter 4

1. Marshall, George C. *Memoirs of My Services in the World War, 1917–1918.* Foreword and notes by James L. Collins Jr. Boston: Houghton Mifflin, 1976, pp. 116–120.

2. Cray, Ed. *General of the Army: George C. Marshall, Soldier and Statesman.* New York: W. W. Norton, 1990, p. 69.

3. Ibid., p. 74.

4. Pogue, Forrest C. *George C. Marshall: Education of a General.* Vol. 1 of 4-vol. biography titled *George C. Marshall.* New York: Viking, 1963, p. 187.

5. Ibid., p. 189.

Chapter 5

1. Pogue, Forrest C. *George C. Marshall: Education of a General.* New York: Viking, 1963, p. 193.

2. Lejeune, Major John A. Letter dated October 25, 1934. VMI Alumni file.

3. *New York Times,* July 20, 1919.

4. Marshall, George C. "National Defense: The Business of Every Citizen," address at Brunswick, Md., November 6, 1938, quoted in Cray, Ed. *General of the Army: George C. Marshall, Soldier and Statesman.* New York: W. W. Norton, 1990, p. 85.

5. Letter from Marshall to Pershing, October 14, 1927. Pershing Papers, Library of Congress.

6. Collins, General J. Lawton. *Lightning Joe: An Autobiography.* Baton Rouge: Louisiana State University Press, 1979, pp. 49–50.

7. Letter from Marshall to Pershing, March 28, 1932. Pershing Papers. Library of Congress.

Chapter 6

1. Marshall, Katherine Tupper. *Together: Annals of an Army Wife.* New York: Tupper and Love, 1946, p. 10.

2. Marshall to Pershing, December 27, 1935. Pershing Papers, Library of Congress.
3. Marshall, *Together: Annals of an Army Wife*, p. 26.

Chapter 7

1. Cray, Ed. *General of the Army: George C. Marshall, Soldier and Statesman.* New York: W. W. Norton, 1990, p. 126.
2. Ibid., p. 241.
3. Pogue, Forrest C. *George C. Marshall: Ordeal and Hope.* Vol. 2 of 4-vol. biography titled *George C. Marshall.* New York: Viking, 1966, p. 209.
4. Cray, *General of the Army*, p. 239.
5. *Pearl Harbor Attack.* Hearings Before the Joint Committee on the Investigation of the Pearl Harbor Attack. Vol. XI. Washington, D.C., 1946, p. 1108.

Chapter 8

1. Eisenhower, Dwight D. *Crusade in Europe.* Garden City, N.Y.: Doubleday, 1948, p. 117.
2. Perry, Mark. *Partners in Command: George Marshall and Dwight Eisenhower in War and Peace.* New York: Penguin, 2007, p. 5.
3. Perry, *Partners in Command*, p. 57.
4. Ibid., p. 23.
5. Ibid., p. 29.
6. Miller, Merle. *Ike the Soldier: As They Knew Him.* New York: G. P. Putnam's Sons, 1987, p. 359.
7. Eisenhower, *Crusade in Europe*, p. 50.

Chapter 9

1. Marshall, Katherine Tupper. *Together: Annals of an Army Wife.* New York: Tupper and Love, 1946, pp. 129–130.
2. Hobbs, Joseph P. *Dear General: Eisenhower's Wartime Letters to Marshall.* Baltimore, Md.: The Johns Hopkins University Press, p. 51.
3. Ibid., p. 59.
4. Marshall, George C. "Remarks of General George C. Marshall." *Political Science Quarterly*, Spring 1942.
5. *New York Times*, January 24, 1943.
6. Sherwood, Robert E. *Roosevelt and Hopkins: An Intimate History.* New York: Harper, 1948, p. 689.
7. Eisenhower, Dwight D. *Crusade in Europe.* Garden City, N.Y.: Doubleday, 1948, p. 215.
8. Bland, Larry I., ed. *George C. Marshall: Interviews and Reminiscences for Forrest C. Pogue.* Lexington, Va.: G. C. Marshall Research Foundation, 1991, p. 616.
9. Cray, Ed. *General of the Army: George C. Marshall, Soldier and Statesman.* New York: W. W. Norton, 1990, p. 381.
10. Hobbs, *Dear General*, p. 111.
11. Biennial Report of the Chief of Staff of the U.S. Army, July 1, 1943, p 38.

Chapter 10

1. Biennial Report of the Chief of Staff of the U.S. Army, July 1, 1943, p. 15–17.

2. Collins, General J. Lawton. *Lightning Joe: An Autobiography.* Baton Rouge: Louisiana State University Press, 1979, p. 150.

3. Perry, Mark. *Partners in Command: George Marshall and Dwight Eisenhower in War and Peace.* New York: Penguin, 2007, p. 194.

4. Stimson, Henry Lewis. Diary, May 25, 1943. Microfilm edition at Yale University Library.

5. Churchill, Winston. *The Hinge of Fate.* Vol. 4 of *The Second World War.* Boston: Houghton Mifflin, 1950, p. 812.

6. Eisenhower, Dwight D. *Crusade in Europe.* Garden City, N.Y.: Doubleday, 1948, p. 167.

7. D'Este, Carlo. *Patton: A Genius for War.* New York: HarperCollins, 1995, p. 495.

8. Marshall, Katherine Tupper. *Together: Annals of an Army Wife.* New York: Tupper and Love, 1946, p. 153.

9. Pogue, Forrest C. *George C. Marshall: Organizer of Victory, 1943–1945.* Vol. 3 of 4-vol. biography titled *George C. Marshall.* New York: Viking, 1973, p. 224.

10. Truscott, Lucian K. Jr. *Command Missions: A Personal Story.* New York: E. P. Dutton, 1954, p. 218.

11. Cray, Ed. *General of the Army: George C. Marshall, Soldier and Statesman.* New York: W. W. Norton, 1990, p. 405.

12. Truscott, *Command Missions,* p. 243.

13. Biennial Report of the Chief of Staff of the U.S. Army, July 1, 1943, p. 50.

Chapter 11

1. Hobbs, Joseph P. *Dear General: Eisenhower's Wartime Letters to Marshall.* Baltimore, Md.: The Johns Hopkins University Press, p. 121.

2. Eisenhower, Dwight D. *Crusade in Europe.* Garden City, N.Y.: Doubleday, 1948, p. 215.

3. Cray, Ed. *General of the Army: George C. Marshall, Soldier and Statesman.* New York: W. W. Norton, 1990, p. 433.

4. Bland, Larry I., ed. *George C. Marshall: Interviews and Reminiscences for Forrest C. Pogue.* Lexington, Va.: G. C. Marshall Research Foundation, 1991, p. 344.

5. Collins, General J. Lawton. *Lightning Joe: An Autobiography.* Baton Rouge: Louisiana State University Press, 1979, pp. 175–178.

6. Marshall, Katherine Tupper. *Together: Annals of an Army Wife.* New York: Tupper and Love, 1946, p. 195.

7. Eisenhower, *Crusade in Europe,* p. 249.

8. "Eisenhower to Marshall," Cable S–52951, June 5, 1944. Records of the Supreme Headquarters, Allied Expeditionary Force. Washington, D.C., National Archives.

9. Cray, *General of the Army,* pp. 453–454.

10. Roosevelt, Franklin D. Presidential radio address, June 6, 1944, reprinted in John Gabriel Hunt, ed. *The Essential Franklin Delano Roosevelt: FDR's Greatest Speeches, Fireside Chats, Messages, and Proclamations* (New York: Gramercy, 1995), p. 307.

Chapter 12

1. Atkinson, Rick. *An Army at Dawn: The War in Africa, 1942–1943.* Vol. 1 of The Liberation Trilogy. New York: Henry Holt, 2002, p. 86.

2. Collins, General J. Lawton. *Lightning Joe: An Autobiography.* Baton Rouge: Louisiana State University Press, 1979, p. 183.

3. Bradley, Omar N. *A Soldier's Story.* New York: Henry Holt, 1951, p. 272.
4. Stimson, Henry Lewis. Diary, June 15, 1944. Microfilm edition at Yale University Library.
5. Collins, *Lightning Joe,* pp. 237–240.
6. Perry, Mark. *Partners in Command: George Marshall and Dwight Eisenhower in War and Peace.* New York: Penguin, 2007, pp. 318–320.
7. Eisenhower, Dwight D. *Crusade in Europe,* Garden City, N.Y.: Doubleday, 1948, p. 278.
8. Bradley, *A Soldier's Story,* p. 377.
9. Marshall, George C. *Biennial Report of the Chief of Staff of the U.S. Army, July 1, 1943,* p. 37.
10. "U.S. at War: Results at Quebec," *Time,* September 25, 1944, http://www.time.com/time/magazine/article/0,9171,791615,00.html; accessed 12/24/2009.

Chapter 13

1. Cray, Ed. *General of the Army: George C. Marshall, Soldier and Statesman.* New York: W. W. Norton, 1990, p. 484.
2. Bradley, Omar N. *A Soldier's Story.* New York: Henry Holt, 1951, p. 447.
3. Parker, Danny S. *Battle of the Bulge: Hitler's Ardennes Offensive, 1944–1945.* New York: Da Capo Press, 2004, pp. 6–19.
4. Bradley, *A Soldier's Story,* p. 450.
5. Eisenhower, John S. D. *The Bitter Woods: The Dramatic Story, Told at All Echelons, from Supreme Command to Squad Leader, of the Crisis That Shook the Western Coalition: Hitler's Surprise Ardennes Offensives.* New York: G. P. Putnam's Sons, 1969, p. 33. Reprinted as *The Bitter Woods: The Battle of the Bulge* (New York: Da Capo Press, 1995).
6. Perry, Mark. *Partners in Command: George Marshall and Dwight Eisenhower in War and Peace.* New York: Penguin, 2007, p. 345.

Chapter 14

1. Marshall, Katherine Tupper. *Together: Annals of an Army Wife.* New York: Tupper and Love, 1946, p. 227.
2. Cray, Ed. *General of the Army: George C. Marshall, Soldier and Statesman.* New York: W. W. Norton, 1990, p. 495.
3. Marshall, *Together,* p. 232.
4. Miller, Merle. *Plain Speaking: An Oral Biography of Harry S. Truman.* New York: Berkley, 1974, p. 169.
5. Marshall, *Together,* p. 236.
6. Bradley, Omar N. *A Soldier's Story.* New York: Henry Holt, 1951, p. 535.
7. Eisenhower, Dwight D. *Crusade in Europe.* Garden City, N.Y.: Doubleday, 1948, pp. 399–401.
8. Cray, *General of the Army,* p. 522; the phrase is a traditional Latin proverb, which the Roman playwright Terence (195/185–159 BC) paraphrased in his *Andria* (*The Girl from Andros*) as "Lovers' quarrels are a renewal of love."
9. Bradley, *A Soldier's Story,* pp. 540–541.
10. Pogue, Forrest C. *George C. Marshall: Organizer of Victory, 1943–1945.* New York: Viking, 1973, pp. 557–558.
11. Ibid., pp. 583–584.

Chapter 15

1. Cray, Ed. *General of the Army: George C. Marshall, Soldier and Statesman.* New York: W. W. Norton, 1990, pp. 535–536.
2. Cray, *General of the Army,* p. 544.
3. Perry, Mark. *Partners in Command: George Marshall and Dwight Eisenhower in War and Peace.* New York: Penguin, 2007, p. 373.
4. Cray, *General of the Army,* p. 573.
5. Acheson, Dean. *Present at the Creation: My Years in the State Department.* New York: W. W. Norton, 1987, p. 219.
6. Ibid., p. 219.
7. Ibid., p. 228.

Chapter 16

1. Cray, Ed. *General of the Army: George C. Marshall, Soldier and Statesman.* New York: W. W. Norton, 1990, p. 685.
2. Cray, *General of the Army,* p. 686.
3. *Congressional Record,* June 14, 1951, p. 6602.
4. Cray, *General of the Army,* 723.
5. Ibid.
6. Cray, *General of the Army,* p. 730.

Index

Byrnes, James F., 136, 153, 174, 176

Cairo Conference (1943), 133–5
Cantigny, battle of (1918), 38–9
Casablanca Conference, 112–13
Central Powers of WWI, 29, 48
Chamberlain, Neville, 84
Chaney, James E., 101–2
chemical weapons, 172–3
Chiang Kai-shek, 133, 175–6, 185
Chief of Staff of U.S. Army (Marshall), ix, 2–3,
    24, 85–91, 93–103, 105–17, 121–40,
    141–51, 153–69, 171–5
  and Army management systems, 96–7, 143
  Army modernization, *See* maneuver warfare
  and Army size, 109
  and chemical weapons, 172–3
  and clarity, 93–4, 98–101
  and commandos, 97–100
  and diplomacy, 135–7, 150, 156
  and the future, 135
  and "integrated arms" approach to warfare, 173
  logistics, 145, 150, 153–4, 157–8
  and manpower, 157–8, 171
  and Normandy invasion, 141–4
  and Operation Torch, 106–7
  and "victory fever," 153–4
  See atomic bomb; Louisiana-Texas maneuvers;
    RAINBOW; unified command
China, ix, x, 1, 63–4, 67, 80, 89, 133, 135,
    175–6, 184, 186–7
China-Burma-India (C-B-I) theater of war, 133
Chinese Civil War, 175–6
Chinese Communists, x, 80, 175–6, 185
Chinese Nationalists, x, 80, 175–6, 185
Churchill, Winston, x, 57–8, 87, 94–7, 102,
    106–7, 109, 112–13, 121–3, 129, 133–4,
    144–5, 149–50, 163, 165–7, 172, 174–6,
    188–9
Civil War, 7, 8, 11, 17, 18, 36, 74, 75, 176, 185
Civilian Conservation Corps (CCC), 74, 77–8,
    80
Clark, Mark Wayne, 80–1, 101, 107, 109, 132,
    134, 138, 141, 145, 165
Clayton, William L., 179
Clemenceau, Georges, 36, 46
Cleveland, Grover, 7
Cocheu, Frank S., 65
Cold War, 62, 85, 177–80
Coles, Edmund, 70
Collier's magazine, 38
Collins, Gladys, 136–7
Collins, James L., 56, 62
Collins Jr., James Lawton, 62
Collins, Joseph Lawton ("Lightning Joe"), 66–7,
    120, 136–7, 142–4, 146–7, 185–6

Columbus, battle of (1916), 28
Combined Chiefs of Staff (WWII), 95, 160
Combined Operations Headquarters (COHQ),
    98, 100
Commandos (Great Britain), 97–100
Communism, 175–7, 184–8
Confederate States of America ("Confederacy"),
    7, 9
Connor, Fox, 41–3, 49–50, 59–61
Coolidge, Calvin, 69, 79
Cota, Norman, 67
Craig, Malin, 1–2, 18–19, 80–1, 83–6
Crusade in Europe, 114, 148
Czechoslovakia, 84
Czolgosz, Leon, 12

Danville Military Institute (Virginia), 12
Darby, William Orlando, 101
Darby's Rangers, 101, 106
de Gaulle, Charles, 144–5
Dern, George, 77
Dewey, Thomas E., 153, 181
Díaz, Porforio, 22
Dill, John, 87
Drum, Hugh A., 50
Duke, Basil, 7

Eastern Task Force, 106
Eden, Anthony, 144
Edward VIII of the United Kingdom, 58
Egypt, 102, 113
Eighth Air Force (U.S.), 24, 109, 124–5
Eighth Army (U.S.), 185
Eighth Army Corps (U.S.), 52
Eighth Infantry Regiment (U.S.), 70–1, 74, 143
Eighty-second Airborne Division (U.S.), 139,
    155
Eisenhower, Dwight D. ("Ike"), 88–9, 94–5,
    97–8, 100–2, 106, 108–14, 116–17, 119,
    122–5, 128–9, 131–9, 141–2, 144, 147,
    149, 153–4, 157, 159–60, 164, 166–9,
    173, 175–6, 180, 185, 188–9
  closing cable of WWII, 169
  commanding general in the ETO, 102
  full general, 116
  president, 188–9
  Supreme Allied Commander, Europe, 95, 135,
    142, 144, 154
  and unified command, 110–11, 144, 155–6
Elizabeth II of United Kingdom, 189
Emmons, Delos C., 120
Erickson, Hjalmar, 50
European Theater of Operations (ETO), 96,
    101–2, 159

Falaise gap, battle of (1944), 148–9